JESUS
ACCORDING TO S. MARK

JESUS ACCORDING TO S. MARK

BY

J. M. THOMPSON

FELLOW AND DEAN OF DIVINITY, S. MARY MAGDALEN COLLEGE, OXFORD
EXAMINING CHAPLAIN TO THE BISHOP OF GLOUCESTER

SECOND EDITION

WIPF & STOCK · Eugene, Oregon

Wipf and Stock Publishers
199 W 8th Ave, Suite 3
Eugene, OR 97401

Jesus According to S. Mark, 2nd Edition
By Thompson, J. M.
Softcover ISBN-13: 978-1-7252-9113-3
Hardcover ISBN-13: 978-1-7252-9112-6
eBook ISBN-13: 978-1-7252-9114-0
Publication date 11/2/2020
Previously published by Methuen & Co., 1910

This edition is a scanned facsimile of
the original edition published in 1910.

CONTENTS

CHAPTER	PAGE
I. Introductory	1
II. Jesus' Family and Friends	16
III. Jesus' Way of Life	41
IV. Jesus' Mind	72
V. Jesus' Social Outlook	109
VI. Jesus' Morality	140
VII. Jesus' Religion	164
VIII. Jesus Himself	198
IX. Conclusion	274
Indexes	281

JESUS ACCORDING TO S. MARK

CHAPTER I

INTRODUCTORY

I

IT would be difficult to find a better starting-point for the present inquiry than the words which stand at the head of the canonical accounts of the life of Jesus. "The Gospel according to S. Mark" suggests clearly enough the nature of the facts and the method of their investigation. It implies that there is one Gospel, and that it is presented in more than one form. It sanctions a distinction between the essential facts and interpretation of facts upon which Christian belief depends, and the partial and more or less accidental presentation of them which survives in the written records of the evangelists. There is a Gospel behind the Gospels: but it is through the Gospels that the Gospel is to be known.

It is therefore not merely a possible and interesting thing to examine the figure of Jesus as it is presented in a particular Gospel : rather it is the natural and proper method of study marked out by the Church's own tradition. Jesus whom the Church confesses and worships is a single person : but his historical figure is the result of a large number of converging experiences : and, from among these, four have been picked out by common instinct and the sanction of use as the most representative, the most true. They were not selected because they corroborated or supplemented one another as parts of an organic whole, but because each one embodied —it might be with apostolic authority—what Christians remembered or believed about their Master. They were based not on official biographies, but on personal memoirs; and they were the productions of men who worked from very different points of view. It follows that much of the originality and force of these early memoirs will be lost if they are habitually read together as one book. Such a method is psychologically and historically false. They should be read as they were written, each as the individual presentation of a common Gospel: and then everything that can be discovered as to their particular standpoints or mutual relations will become a help and not a hindrance to the proper understanding of them.

II

Christianity claims to be a "historical religion" in a special sense. It believes itself to be, from beginning to end, a continuous and consistent whole. No facts could be simpler, at first sight, than those in which it takes its rise; no organisation more complex, no growth of creed and ritual more luxuriant, than that in which it ends. But the beginning is held to include the end, as the seed includes the flower; and the end is held to be valid because, and so far as, it follows from the beginning. Jesus the centre of Catholic worship is Jesus "the prophet from Nazareth of Galilee". No thought may be held or spoken of him now which might not have been held or spoken of him then. No theory of Church or Sacrament is true which is not faithful to its charter of historical facts. Conversely, no doubt, if Christian faith is meaningless without the Christian facts, so are the Christian facts without Christian faith. But just as Jesus whom the Church confesses must be known chiefly by the faith that worships, so Jesus of Galilee must be known chiefly by the science that investigates. In a word, Jesus of the whole experience of Christian life must be one who satisfies not only the needs of the religious sense, but also the canons of historical criticism. This is the specific claim of Christianity—truth of faith and truth of fact as inextricable elements in truth of religion.

It is therefore possible and right to apply scientific method to the investigation of the figure of Jesus. But, when this is granted, it becomes very necessary to point out the limits within which such a method is valid, and the kinds of conclusion which may be expected to follow from it.

Christians believe that a certain person lived and died; that certain events took place in relation to him; that his character and claims were of a certain kind. But this belief has been and is variously expressed. Its most primitive and universal expression takes the form not of a collection of documents, but of a way of life.[1] The Christian society, with its creeds and ministry

[1] Acts ix. 2; xviii. 25, 26; xix. 9, 23; xxii. 4; xxiv. 14, 22.

INTRODUCTORY

and worship and life of charity, ought to be, and for the most part has been, the truest witness to Jesus, and the one most after his own heart.

Again, the intimate memories of this society, the evangelical tradition which it kept alive in the world, has for the most part passed away into silence. It is only a small remnant of its witness which has survived in the very imperfect medium of written documents. The Gospels are little more than islands from which one can hazard a guess as to the course of mountain ranges below the level of sight. But a document has a value which is all its own. Unwritten tradition is at the mercy of a memory which forgets, and of a will which wishes to believe. Custom and ritual crystallise mistakes. There is an easy transition from creed to mythology. The Christian documents have a unique value for correction, for corroboration, for proof; and no work will be wasted that leads to a better understanding of their meaning.

The first aim of scientific method, in dealing with the Christian documents, will be to construct a genealogical table of manuscripts. This is the primary work of textual criticism; and although those who have worked longest at the problem will be the last to claim finality for the conclusions which have been reached, we may assume that a text trustworthy enough for all practical purposes has now been established.[1]

The second aim will be to reproduce as far as possible the stages in the growth of the Christian story; to show which parts of the record are most original, and which have been derived; to sift the qualities of evidence, and to disentangle the strands of tradition. This is more particularly the work of literary and historical criticism. It is more difficult than purely textual investigation; and its results are correspondingly tentative; but it at any rate gives working hypotheses for dealing with the documents.

III

Putting aside the Old Testament, which derives a Christian interpretation through the New Testament, the Christian documents fall under three heads—Gospels, Acts, and Epistles. Of these groups only the first claims to deal directly with the life and character of Jesus; but it will

---

[1] For the sake of the convenience of being able to quote a recognised English translation, the text used in this book is the Greek Testament with the readings adopted by the Revisers of the Authorised Version.

be advisable to indicate shortly what amount of evidence is also available from the other groups, in order to clear the ground for the exclusive treatment of one gospel which is to follow.

The central group of Epistles, which is by common consent both early and authentic—the group consisting of 1 and 2 Corinthians, Galatians and Romans—might well be called, "The Gospel according to S. Paul". It embodies the one Gospel; and it presents it from an individual point of view. But in so far as its tone is primarily theological, not historical, it is a gospel of the type of S. John rather than of S. Mark. Only at two points does it deal deliberately with the same subject matter as the gospels—in S. Paul's account of the institution of the Eucharist,[1] and in his summary of the evidence for the appearances of Jesus after the Resurrection.[2] For the rest, it must always remain something of a puzzle, that the correspondence of a man to whom Jesus was the source of religious inspiration and the great reality of life should have so little to say about Jesus' human life. It is, of course, true that the letters are occasional, not systematic; that they assume a common background of facts as well as of faith; that the attention of Christians

[1] 1 Cor. xi. 23.   [2] xv. 3.

was fixed less upon Jesus who had once been in the world, than upon Jesus who would soon visit it again ; and that in the absence of written records S. Paul may really have been ignorant of all but the outlines of the life and death of Jesus. At any rate, one gathers from his epistles the main facts of the Gospel story and no more ; so that if this were all the evidence of S. Paul's standpoint, one might be tempted to regard him as a ringleader of the sect of the Modernists, whose dogmatic certainties rested upon a very flimsy basis of facts.

That S. Paul's position was not, however, peculiar to himself, but rather part of the attitude of the early Church as a whole, is seen from a consideration of the Acts. The later chapters of this book, since they deal mainly with events in the life of S. Paul, and are admittedly the work of one who was his fellow-traveller, may be expected to share the point of view of the Epistles, And this, as a matter of fact, is the case. With the exception of a solitary saying[1]—the only word of Jesus which has survived in the New Testament independently of the gospels—nothing is added to our knowledge of the Gospel story, and only its main outlines are corroborated. The

[1] Acts xx. 35.

INTRODUCTORY

earlier chapters, with their frequent summaries of early Christian sermons, might be expected to throw much light upon the subject. But, interesting and important as they are as evidence corroborative of the point of view of the earliest Gospel traditions, they cannot be said to add any new knowledge about Jesus. "Jesus of Nazareth, a man approved of God unto you by mighty works and wonders and signs;"[1] "His Servant Jesus . . . the Holy and Righteous One . . . the Prince of Peace;"[2] "Thy holy Servant Jesus, whom thou didst anoint;"[3] "Jesus, whom ye slew, hanging him on a tree"[4]—all such references fall within the Gospel tradition, so far as their facts go; what novelty there is belongs to the language of primitive Christian devotion. More detailed, and of special interest through the traditional relationship between the Petrine "memoirs" and the Gospel according to S. Mark, is S. Peter's speech before Cornelius: "The word which he sent unto the children of Israel, preaching good tidings of peace by Jesus Christ (he is Lord of all)—that saying ye yourselves know, which was published throughout all Judæa,

[1] Acts ii. 22.   [2] iii. 13, 14.
[3] iv. 27.   [4] v. 30.

beginning from Galilee, after the baptism which John preached; even Jesus of Nazareth, how that God anointed him with the Holy Ghost and with power: who went about doing good, and healing all that were oppressed of the devil; for God was with him. And we are witnesses of all things which he did both in the country of the Jews and in Jerusalem."[1] Here the Apostle goes behind the final scenes of the gospel, which seem generally to have absorbed the attention of the early Church, and corroborates in a most significant way the point of view and subject matter of the second gospel. But, again, there is nothing new.

Thus we are thrown back upon the gospels, which still supply what they were no doubt originally compiled to supply, a permanent record of the manner of Jesus' life among men. Strange as it may seem, this was a subject which did not greatly interest the first generation of Christians; and there was some danger, then as now, lest the plain facts of Jesus' historical Incarnation should be overlaid and obscured by theories born of his supernatural presence in the Church. This need of laying stress upon the real humanity of Jesus, as the security of a

[1] Acts x. 36-39.

INTRODUCTORY

true Incarnation, is a marked feature in the fourth gospel, which in some other respects may be so sharply contrasted with the Synoptic Gospels. But before the memory of the facts was lost, and while it was still possible to take an unsophisticated view of the manner of the Incarnation, the earlier forms of the gospels, at any rate, were compiled; and it is thus possible, to a great extent, to get behind the Christology and soteriology of the Church to Jesus as he lived among men, and healed and taught them.

It will appear from what has been said about the fourth gospel, that we cannot regard it as historical evidence of the same kind as the other gospels. In spite of its insistence upon the true humanity of Jesus, and in spite of the vivid appearance of historical detail which is so perplexing an element in it, yet one feels that these things are no more than the setting of something which is not a biography, but a treatise in theology; and that its author would be almost as ready to sacrifice historical truth where it clashes with his dogmatic purpose as he is (apparently) anxious to observe it where it illustrates his point. This does not destroy, indeed it probably enhances, the importance of the book from other points of view; but it greatly lessens its value for the purposes of such an inquiry as the present.

The outstanding feature of the remaining gospels is that, although each has a character of its own, and individuality of treatment and style, yet quite clearly, in point of subject matter, they are not independent. There is one large element which is common to all three gospels; and there is another which is common to the first and third. If the gospels were mere compilations, no further question might arise; we might abstract the "triple tradition," and deny any further relationship. But the matter is not so simple. Textual criticism shows that unity of editorship holds throughout each gospel, and that the common tradition undergoes variation accordingly. So it becomes essential to determine the nature of the relationship within the synoptic group. Did X borrow the common matter from Y, and Y from Z? or did both X and Y derive it from Z? or did X, Y and Z take it independently from a fourth original? Not very long ago it would have been assumed that the second gospel was a weakened and summarised edition of the first; but a better criticism has revolutionised the early conclusions, and it is now generally agreed that S. Matthew and S. Luke independently used

INTRODUCTORY

and edited either our S. Mark's Gospel or something very like it. It is also admitted that there must have been a second source common to S. Matthew and S. Luke but unknown to S. Mark; and this is commonly conjectured to have been a document, called for sake of convenience, "Q". In addition to these main sources of material there were many special traditions known to one or another of the evangelists. Thus, some passages seem to be original parts of S. Mark, which were for various reasons omitted by S. Matthew and S. Luke; others, again, seem to be genuine traditions not known to S. Mark, but recovered by the later evangelists; a few, doubtless, represent later additions or interpretations of less value. Thus, on the simplest hypothesis, which science always prefers to the more elaborate, it ought to be possible to assign the greater part of the gospels with some certainty to one or other of these layers of tradition, and to arrive at an adequately scientific method of study.

IV

It remains to justify the exclusive treatment of the second gospel. From what has been said as to the relations between the synoptic writers it would appear that both the source of the "triple tradition" and the hypothetical document called "Q" must be of a very primitive nature. If the question of their relative antiquity be raised, one can only say that, whilst no literary dependance can be proved between "Q" and S. Mark, the balance of argument favours the priority of the "triple tradition". For one will be inclined to think that a tradition which records in very simple style acts and short sayings is more primitive than one which consists of more elaborate and independent teaching.

In addition to the simplicity, the vividness, and naturalness which are the obvious features of the second gospel, there is the well-known and very credible tradition that S. Mark was the "interpreter" of S. Peter, and recorded in this gospel what that Apostle remembered of the life and death of his Master. In any case one is justified in considering this document as of unique historical value: it probably represents as a whole an authentic account of a very early stratum of Christian tradition about the life and character of Jesus. More was discovered by later inquiry: the outlines were filled up, the bare facts were interpreted, the necessary developments of faith and worship soon began. The latest, not the

INTRODUCTORY

earliest, account of Jesus should be the most perfect, the most akin to the complex needs of men. But without the sketch the picture would have been impossible. And the more one studies this early record, the more convinced one becomes that it is a true biography, in which no essential part of the figure has been left out, and nothing is obviously disproportionate or out of drawing. The Jesus of S. Mark lives and moves and has real being: he is vivid, characteristic, complete. As one learns more about S. Francis from the imperfect "Speculum" of Brother Leo than from the official biography of S. Bonaventura, so one hopes to find in this personal account, however unfinished it may be, a more vivid and tangible Jesus than in the completer and more laboured records.

One last word of introduction. It is not denied here that some beliefs, which might be called the rudiments of the Apostles' Creed, were in the minds of the Evangelists. But S. Mark's gospel, at any rate, does not base its appeal upon those beliefs. And if, whilst written by and for Christians, it could take up this detached position, it can be read by Christians in the same spirit.

CHAPTER II

JESUS' FAMILY AND FRIENDS

I

THE method which we have prescribed for ourselves exempts us from the need of stating those *a priori* considerations which so often prejudice as well as preface an *a posteriori* argument. Thus we need say nothing of the "fulness of time," of the long preparation for, and world-wide setting of the Incarnation. Jesus and his contemporaries knew nothing of all this. Even if they had been conscious of it, we should be able to reach it best through their evidence. Again, there is no need to state the general condition of Jewish society and religion under which Jesus grew up, and which he took for granted. We shall most profitably consider them through his reactions upon them.

We shall not limit our inquiry, either positively or negatively, by the Catholic creeds. The definitions of the creeds claim to be the necessary outcome not merely of meditative but also of scientific study. If the creeds are true, they have nothing to fear from the sound application of scientific method to any matter in heaven or earth. We shall not presuppose them, because we have faith that they will be found waiting at the end of the argument. To reverse this process would be to doubt the creeds and to prejudice the whole method of argument.

We shall beware of the similar error of reading into the actual data of the Incarnation *a priori* ideas as to what the Incarnation must have involved. This is the cardinal mistake of the Apocryphal Gospels, which often seem to deal with the childhood of Jesus on a preconceived theory of the nature of his divinity. It is the error which in subtler forms predisposes every one who studies the character of Jesus to distort it in the interests of his particular social or national prejudices. Rénan's Jesus seems to Englishmen intolerably French: the Jesus whom we preach to the Chinese seems to them, far too often, a glorified European.

It may not be possible wholly to avoid these errors; but we shall try to deal with the evidence as it comes, interpreting it as simply as may be, from the point of view of those by whom or for whom it was first compiled, and endeavouring to distinguish what is original from what is derived, what is strongly from what is weakly witnessed, what is solid fact from what is flimsy interpretation.

II

"And it came to pass in those days, that Jesus came from Nazareth of Galilee, and was baptised of John in the Jordan":[1] such, by common consent of the three evangelists, was the first emergence of Jesus into public view. S. Matthew and S. Luke, who have prefixed long narratives of the birth and childhood of Jesus, make a fresh start with the preaching of the Baptist. It is here that S. Luke introduces his most elaborate indication of the date.[2]

Jesus not only comes from Nazareth; he *is of* Nazareth: no other home or birthplace is ever hinted at by S. Mark. The unclean spirit at Capernaum, the crowd of Jesus' followers, the high priest's servant at Jerusalem, the young man at the open tomb—all agree as to this title, "Jesus of Nazareth," or "Jesus the Nazarene".[3]

---

[1] Mark i. 9. [2] Matt. iii. 1, Luke iii. 1.
[3] Mark i. 24, x. 47, xiv. 67, xvi. 6. (The Greek word Ναζαρηνός is the same in each case.)

JESUS' FAMILY AND FRIENDS

But what lies behind? Jesus is already in the prime of life:[1] is the record of the thirty years completely closed?

To the first generation of Christians this was, apparently, a subject of little interest. The earliest tradition has nothing to record of the long time before the baptism. That was the beginning of Christian experience for the disciples, as it was very possibly of Messianic consciousness for Jesus himself. But, before very long, interest began to be aroused. As the hope of Jesus' second presence in the world grew dim, the nature of his first appearance became more important. Old stories were revived, new evidence, perhaps, discovered: birth-narratives and childhood-narratives were written: and from a mass of such literature, if one may judge by the parallel case of the gospels, two accounts came to be accepted as orthodox and canonical—the narratives that are prefixed to the Gospels according to S. Matthew and S. Luke.

It is not within our scope to deal with the controversies which circle round these stories. But there is one line of argument which springs

---

[1] Luke iii. 23. *Cf.* John viii. 57—apparently a different tradition.

directly from the second gospel, and which therefore calls for consideration. It is this: What is the evidential value of the silence of S. Mark as to the birth and childhood of Jesus? This is not so simple a question as it might at first seem to be. S. Mark's silence, were that all, might be accounted for on a number of grounds—ignorance of what was not generally known at the time when he wrote; lack of interest in what was not yet considered important; a historical purpose which limited itself to the public ministry of Jesus; or dependence upon the scope of S. Peter's personal experience. But the difficulty lies here: S. Mark is not merely silent about Jesus' birth and childhood. Explicitly he says nothing; but he implies a good deal. It is well-nigh impossible to begin a biography at the age of thirty without throwing back some light upon the years that have gone before. And S. Mark's Gospel is no exception to this rule. What, then, is the nature of S. Mark's witness to the birth and childhood of Jesus?

III

The appearance of Jesus at John's baptism, which is marked by special signs of spiritual

JESUS' FAMILY AND FRIENDS

stress and fervour,[1] was followed by a period of retirement, and meditation, and struggle against temptation. During all this time, the length of which we cannot very well determine, one supposes Jesus to have stayed away from his own country, and from his home at Nazareth. It was not till "John was delivered up" that he "came into Galilee, preaching the gospel of God, and saying, The time is fulfilled, and the kingdom of God is at hand: repent ye, and believe in the gospel".[2] There follows that first period of preaching in the parts of Galilee near Capernaum, and along the lake-side, which is marked by extraordinary popular demonstrations—by crowds which follow and throng Jesus and his disciples—and which culminates in an occasion, apparently at S. Peter's house in Capernaum, where "the multitude cometh together again, so that they could not so much as eat bread".[3]

It is at this moment that we are introduced for the first time to Jesus' relations and friends. The strange doings of the new prophet by the lake-side are reported in all the hill-country

---

[1] *E.g.* the repeated "straightway" of Mark i. 10, 12; the "driveth" of i. 12; and the agency of the Spirit throughout the passage.

[2] Mark i. 14, 15.   [3] iii. 20.

above the lake, and before long they come to the ears of Jesus' friends and neighbours at Nazareth. It is an interesting, almost a critical moment. Will the people of Nazareth be proud of their native prophet, and welcome his popularity as the public recognition of merits long known to themselves? or will they depreciate his powers and achievements through the familiarity which breeds contempt? The course which they actually take is neither of these. "And when his friends heard it, they went out to lay hold on him: for they said, he is beside himself."[1] The words occur only in S. Mark: but there is little reason to doubt that they belong to the original tradition, when one considers how commonly statements which might be thought unedifying or unorthodox are modified or omitted by S. Matthew and S. Luke, and when one finds the former process actually going on in the reading of *Codex Bezae*—"And when the scribes and the rest heard about him, they came forth to seize him, for they said, *he is driving the people mad*". There was, then, no question as to approval or disapproval of Jesus' new popularity: his friends simply thought that he must be mad. And the natural inference from

[1] Mark iii. 21. "Friends" (οἱ παρ' αὐτοῦ) probably means "relatives".

this is, that there had been nothing in Jesus' life up to this point which would lead his friends to anticipate or understand his ministry. They had never expected anything of this kind: he must be out of his senses to act so.

It is true that the point which chiefly offended Jesus' friends, if one may judge from the position of the incident in S. Mark's narrative, was the publicity of his proceedings: but it remains a safe inference that nothing in his thirty years of home life had prepared them for his present authority of word and act.[1]

It has also been suggested that Jesus' relatives were all the time at Capernaum, living in the same house as himself, and that they only came out of the house to restrain him when the devotion of the crowd grew to an unusual pitch. But probably (1) what has been said about Jesus coming into Capernaum and lodging with Peter holds good: his mother and brethren would not be living away from home, or in another man's house. (2) "He is beside himself" in any case justifies the main point that we are trying to make. (3) Jesus' disowning of his family fits in with this view.

S. Mark puts in close proximity to this inci-

---

[1] Mark i. 22, 27; *cf.* ii. 12.

dent another which is very similar to it, and may even be a continuation of it. "And there came his mother and his brethren; and, standing without, they sent unto him, calling him."[1] This is the only direct mention of Jesus' mother in S. Mark's Gospel:[2] she comes, apparently, on the same errand as the friends just before—to induce her son to return home: she is met by what is not merely a great profession of the spiritual kinship of all God's servants, but also a literal renunciation of the claims of family relationship.[3] Yet Mary must have known the circumstances of Jesus' birth; must have anticipated, if any one could, the time when he would begin to do his Father's business; must have been able to understand the enthusiasm that made him first an outcast from his family and then the rejected of his nation. Unless S. Mark is wrong in the position, and, by implication, the meaning which he assigns to this incident, it is difficult not to infer that Jesus' mother and brothers shared the point of view of his friends, and had not been led by anything in his previous life to anticipate his present state of mind.

The third incident which must be compared

[1] Mark iii. 31.   [2] *Cf.* vi. 3.   [3] iii. 34, 35.

with these is the visit which Jesus pays to "His own country," when he preaches in the synagogue at Nazareth. It is not clear what is the relation of this narrative to the two last: nothing is said of his friends' or relations' attempts to bring Jesus home: he comes of his own accord, and moves among the villagers as though for the first time. "And many hearing him were astonished, saying, Whence hath this man these things? and, What is the wisdom that is given unto this man, and what mean such mighty works wrought by his hands?"[1] Jesus had perhaps preached before in the village synagogue; but never with this wisdom: he had passed daily among the sick and halt and blind; but had done no such works as were now reported of him. And then the village gossip becomes more personal. "Is not this the carpenter, the son of Mary, and brother of James, and Joses, and Judas, and Simon? and are not his sisters here with us?"[2] Jesus acknowledges "his own kin," and seems to see no inconsistency between the old life and the new. But to those who had known at any rate the externals of his thirty years' life among them, his new powers and

[1] Mark vi. 2.   [2] vi. 3.

claims were quite incredible, "and they were offended in him".[1]

It is not easy to estimate the exact force of this evidence. But that it amounts to something more than silence upon the question of Jesus' birth, and of the nature of his early life, can hardly be denied. The attitude of his fellow-townsmen towards Jesus certainly excludes the theory of the childhood which is illustrated by the Apocryphal Gospels. It also seems hard to reconcile with the miraculous or unusual events surrounding the Nativity in the stories prefixed to the first and third gospels. But these points demand separate investigation, such as cannot be given to them here.

There is, however, one other passage which throws some light on the subject, and that from the most significant point of view, namely Jesus' own knowledge about his birth. In the course of his teaching during the last week of his life Jesus propounded a question with regard to the 110th Psalm. The common interpretation of the

[1] This perhaps bears on the last incident in implying that Jesus' mother and brothers have left Nazareth, whereas the sisters are still there. But one might still suppose that they had left in order to fetch Jesus home, and had then settled in Capernaum.

JESUS' FAMILY AND FRIENDS

Psalm represented it as Messianic—its author, David, in it addressing the Messiah, the Son of David. Jesus urges that since David calls the Messiah "Lord," the Messiah cannot really be his son.[1] Now he had on previous occasions accepted the title "Son of David" in its conventional Messianic sense. But he had never used it of himself. And now it appears that he has some reason for wishing to argue that, although not David's son, he may yet be the Messiah. That is to say, Jesus did not think himself to be descended from David, as the genealogies given by S. Matthew and S. Luke assert to have been the case. Either, then, these genealogies are based on a misapprehension, or Jesus was mistaken. But if Jesus had grounds for not believing himself to be descended from David, what were they? Did he know that Joseph was a descendant of David, but that he was not Joseph's son? Or was he ignorant of Joseph's descent, and of the enrolment at Bethlehem by which S. Luke corroborates it?

On the whole, the former alternative, if one must choose between the two, seems to be the more likely: in which case we seem to obtain

[1] Mark xii. 35-37.

evidence from the earliest Gospel anticipating some such story as that of the Virgin birth.

There is, however, a third alternative. Since those who called Jesus "Son of David" used the words in the conventional Messianic sense and not from any special knowledge of his actual descent—since, that is, those who might have known it seem to have been unaware of Joseph's Davidic genealogy—we may prefer to think that the first and third gospels are wrong and that Jesus is here urging his human parentage as an argument against his Davidic descent.

IV

Further evidence as to the things which lie behind Jesus' first public ministry might be looked

---

[1] The description of Jesus as "the carpenter," together with the absence of any mention of Joseph, suggests that the latter was dead, and that Jesus, as the eldest son, had carried on the family trade. If this were so, it would help to account for the indignation of his brethren with one who, by becoming a preacher, had left them to support the family. And the phrase "Son of Mary" would perhaps be natural if Joseph were no longer alive, and need not have a dogmatic sense. S. Matthew, apparently disliking the slur implied in "the carpenter," puts "the carpenter's son," and S. Luke says "Joseph's son" (Matt. xiii. 55, Luke iv. 22) thereby suggesting a new difficulty—the acceptance by the evangelists of the villagers' idea of Jesus' paternity. Of this S. Mark knows nothing.

JESUS' FAMILY AND FRIENDS

for in the attitude of his chosen friends, the disciples. Nothing could at first sight be more surprising than the unquestioning trust with which the earliest companions of Jesus obeyed his call: without a moment's hesitation, "they left the nets, and followed him"; or "they left their father Zebedee in the boat with the hired servants, and went after him".[1] Was this really their first meeting? It is almost impossible to suppose so. S. Luke tries to meet this difficulty by prefixing to the call the story of the miraculous draught of fishes,[2] and the incident of the healing of S. Peter's mother-in-law[3]—both rather obvious misplacements. Assuming that S. Mark's narrative is correct, so far as it goes, we are driven to ask whether we can infer anything as to what lies behind the first definite call of the apostles.

Nazareth was too far from the lake to make it likely that Jesus was often able to go there. But if Salome, the wife of Zebedee, and the mother of James and John, was a sister of Mary of Nazareth,[4] it is very probable that Jesus had

[1] Mark i. 18, 20. [2] Luke v. 1. [3] Luke iv. 38.
[4] This is probably the true interpretation of John xix. 25; and it throws some light on the incident in Mark x. 35-40.

at least this point of contact with the fishermen of Galilee—that he had stayed with his cousins, had helped them in their work, and had come to know others engaged in the same pursuit. Among these were two brothers, Simon and Andrew—the former a married man, the latter apparently unmarried—living with Simon's mother-in-law in a house at Capernaum. From the way in which Simon's house is open, not only to Jesus, but also to James and John,[1] and becomes the only home in Jesus' wandering life,[2] it is natural to think that the formal call was the outcome rather than the beginning of the friendship with Simon and Andrew. One may perhaps argue in a similar way from the ready hospitality of Levi[3] to some degree of previous acquaintance; though the evidence is weaker in this case. And it is probable that longer experience as well as deeper insight qualified S. Peter, S. James and S. John to be the inner circle of the disciples, who alone were allowed to be with Jesus at the supreme moments of his spiritual life.

On the whole then, one may infer some pre-

[1] Mark i. 29.
[2] ii. 1, iii. 19, ix. 33, x. 10. As to the nature of the house, *cf.* ii. 4.
[3] ii. 15.

vious sympathy and companionship as the background of the sudden "call" of the first disciples. But there is little or nothing to be learnt from this source as to the nature of Jesus' pre-baptismal life. The disciples accepted and trusted him as he was, asking no questions. The deepest friendships may exist between those who know very little of each other's family history, or external circumstances. In Jesus' case, too, there was added to this the sense that by his renunciation of his family, and baptism, and public preaching, a barrier had been fixed between the old life and the new. Perhaps Jesus was as unwilling to speak as the disciples were to inquire about it.

V

The one friendship which, if it could be established, would throw most light upon the early life of Jesus, is that between himself and John the Baptist. It is clear that the Baptist's preaching was the historical antecedent of Jesus' ministry. It is very possible that Jesus' baptism was the occasion of his "call"—the moment at which he first became aware of his divine sonship, and applied to himself the Messianic language of Isaiah.[1] The discussion with the

[1] Mark i. 11.

disciples after the Transfiguration seems to show that it was the realisation that the Baptist was Elijah, the forerunner of the Messiah, which gave Jesus the clue to the thirty years' puzzle of his own personality.[1] The vision and voice at the baptism were the proof of the great hypothesis which had drawn him into the desert to seek John. Again, the point of the retort with which he meets the challenge of his authority is the very same : if John's baptism is from heaven, then *a fortiori* his own authority is divine : the two stand or fall together.[2]

Further, Jesus seems to have regarded himself, at any rate in the early times of his ministry, as carrying on the work of the Baptist. It is when John is thrown into prison that he begins to preach : his first Gospel is stated in almost the same terms as John's :[3] and he thinks it wise to withdraw for a time from public ministry upon the report of the death of the Baptist.[4] From the Baptist comes the rite of baptism, and the asceticism of the first Christian "rule".[5] Though by degrees the differences between Jesus' preaching and the Baptist's became marked, even profound, there is at any rate some

[1] Mark ix. 11-13.   [2] xi. 27-33.   [3] i. 14, 15.
[4] vi. 30, 31 (taken in connection with the preceding passage).   [5] vi. 8, 9.

JESUS' FAMILY AND FRIENDS

reason for thinking that their earlier religious ideas were not of wholly independent growth.

Whether we can go further than this, and reconstruct a youthful friendship between Jesus and the Baptist, is a question that must be decided upon other evidence than that of S. Mark. There is no direct mention in the second Gospel of any previous acquaintance. But S. Luke seems to allow, if not to indicate, something of the sort, when he describes the family relationship of Mary and Elizabeth, the friendship of the households of Nazareth and of the "city of Judah" in the hill country, and the prenatal sympathy of the two children.[1] So far as S. Mark's implications go, they point in the same direction.

VI

Where relations are incredulous and friends silent or uninterested, one does not expect to learn much from the attitude of the crowd. Certainly no new evidence emerges, unless it be the complete absence of any personal charges, any discreditable reminiscences, such as Jesus' enemies would have been only too willing to bring up against him. Generally speaking, the attitude of the crowd was that of the disciples:

[1] Luke i. 36, 39-41.

they were too much absorbed in his present claims and powers to be interested in his past.

If we try to reconstruct the home circle and the village life from which such wonderful things have sprung, we are met at the outset by a great difficulty. We are introduced to the family life of Jesus, so far as the second Gospel is concerned, at the very moment when the claims of religion have broken it up. The father is dead, the mother is repudiated, the brothers have left their home, only the sisters, married or unmarried, still live in the neighbourhood.[1] There must have been an earlier stage of pious happy family life; but nothing of it now remains. And to Jesus, at any rate, who renounced it, this life must have seemed more of a hindrance than a help to the true service of God. It had taught him the power of prayer, and a profound knowledge of the Scriptures: it had given him keen sympathies, and the simplicity that comes from country life: he had learnt to look below the social surface, and to see the native goodness of men's hearts—the strength of the fisherman, the woman's love, the faith of the child, the humility of the publican and the sinner. But at any moment this life might become a barrier between the soul

[1] A rather precarious inference from the language of Mark vi. 3.

and God : and for Jesus himself the moment had come, and the barrier was ruthlessly broken down.

VII

The weight of the evidence which we have so far collected is cumulative. One feels from quite a number of aspects the significance of S. Mark's silences, and the force of his implications. Even if the second gospel stood alone, we should be able to say something of value as to the earlier parts of Jesus' life. Can we now fill up this outline a little more from a class of evidence that has not yet been investigated? One of the surest signs of a man's upbringing and way of life is his habitual turn of mind and manner of speech. That evidence is often the strongest which does not know itself to be evidential. In the instinctive forms into which they cast their ideas men constantly bear unconscious witness to the influences that have moulded their lives. Jesus, indeed, seems to have overclimbed the ordinary limitations of sympathy and language : but his style was entirely his own ; and for metaphor and imagery he constantly drew upon the matter of his own experience. It is here that he tells us about his past life, by the unconscious witness of habitual speech.

The instances here given are all taken from Jesus' own words as given in the second gospel, These, and other instances like them, are commonly taken as evidence of the keen observation of S. Mark. They are much more valuable as indications of the experiences of Jesus himself.

Some of the commonest ideas belong to the everyday affairs of family life, and represent memories of the home at Nazareth—the patching of old clothes,[1] the proper treatment of wineskins,[2] the use of a lamp,[3] or of salt,[4] the cup of water given to the wayfarer,[5] and the hours spent on the housetop, or in the field.[6] The measure, the millstone, the pitcher of water[7] were all familiar things: and there is doubtless a reminiscence of family ailments, and of the medical lore of the village, not only in the methods of healing adopted by Jesus and his disciples, but also in the prescription of food for one who is weak after long illness,[8] and the popular physiology which underlies the teaching about defilement.[9] Similarly Jesus has the insight to single out from the "tribulation" of the fall of Jerusalem the troubles of "them that are with child and them that give suck in those days"—particularly if it be winter time.[10]

[1] Mark ii. 21.   [2] ii. 22.   [3] iv. 21.   [4] ix. 50.
[5] ix. 41.   [6] xiii. 15, 16.   [7] iv. 24, ix. 42, xiv. 13.
[8] v. 43.   [9] vii. 18, 19.   [10] xiii. 17, 18.

JESUS' FAMILY AND FRIENDS

Village interests and experiences seem to underlie other parts of Jesus' imagery. The bridegroom and the "sons of the bride-chamber,"[1] the robber who breaks his way into a house, pinions the owner, and steals his goods,[2] the outraged guest who shakes off the dust of his feet outside the inhospitable door,[3] the cross, the cruel Roman method of execution,[4] the young colt tied in the village gateway,[5] the dress, salutations, and seats of the scribes,[6] the porter who guards the house when the great man is away on his travels,[7] and the robber against whom the country-side goes out with swords and staves, to seize him[8]—these are not second-hand ideas, or literary "local colour," but the fruit of real experiences—the sights and sounds of village life, the instinctive medium of Jesus' thoughts.

Nor can one doubt Jesus' knowledge of and sympathy with country life, when one considers how habitually he uses the language and ideas of the country-side. Some of his deepest spiritual teaching is connected with the primal mystery of natural growth. God's word in men's hearts is like seed in the field—its growth

---

[1] Mark ii. 19.   [2] iii. 27.   [3] vi. 11.
[4] viii. 34.   [5] xi. 2.   [6] xii. 38, 39.
[7] xiii. 34.   [8] xiv. 48.

dependent on the same influences of heat and moisture and soil:[1] the kingdom of God springs as suddenly from insignificant beginnings as the mustard seed:[2] or it grows gradually and unobserved, "as if a man should cast seed upon the earth; and should sleep and rise night and day, and the seed should spring up and grow, he knoweth not how. The earth beareth fruit of herself; first the blade, then the ear, then the full corn in the ear."[3] Again, Jesus knows that, although April is not the season for figs, a fig tree prematurely in leaf might be expected to have fruit upon it not too unripe to eat;[4] and he draws an effective parable from his knowledge of the same tree: "when her branch is now become tender, and putteth forth its leaves, ye know that summer is nigh; even so ye also, when ye see these things coming to pass, know that he is nigh, even at the doors".[5] So, too, his choice of Isaiah's imagery of the vineyard for a parable of his own rejection[6] shows more than literary plagiarism: his ideas naturally express themselves in the symbols of the countryside.

Some hints remain unclassified. Popular pro-

---

[1] Mark iv. 3-9. [2] iv. 31, 32. [3] iv. 26-28.
[4] xi. 12-14. [5] xiii. 28, 29. [6] xii. 1.

verbs, like that of the camel and the needle's eye,[1] colour many of Jesus' sayings. And he seems to take over the natural portents of the prophecies of Isaiah and Daniel[2] in the spirit of one who interprets them literally, according to the crude astronomy and meteorology of the village mind.

VIII

Individually, these things are details, and of varying importance. But the method of argument which they are meant to illustrate is a sound one, and the cumulative results, at least, are significant. The Incarnation means at any rate this, that Jesus shared naturally and unreservedly the normal interests and ideas of the village people of Nazareth—their tastes and their distastes, their knowledge and their ignorance, their ordinary turn of mind and habitual outlook upon life. Sufficient allowance is not generally made for this consideration. The human nature of Jesus, though admitted as an abstract principle, is but grudgingly conceded in concrete particulars. Yet such a policy impoverishes the Incarnation. And in trying to

[1] Mark x. 25. [2] xiii. 24-27.

understand the meaning of Jesus' Divinity the only right method is not to abstract from his humanity, but to frame some hypothesis which will take it all into account.

CHAPTER III

JESUS' WAY OF LIFE

I

BY common consent of the three evangelists, two great experiences lay between the old life of Jesus and the new. The Baptism sealed the renunciation of home, and proved the hypothesis of the Messiahship: the Temptation determined the method of the Ministry.

It was the realisation that John was Elijah the forerunner, re-incarnate, which discovered Jesus to himself. He underwent John's baptism, so far as we can tell from the earliest tradition, in the spirit in which so many others underwent it, that is, as a rite of preparation for the Kingdom of Heaven, signifying death to sin, and birth to a new life.[1] But he came with a special sense of spiritual crisis, asking for an answer to the problem of his own personality.

[1] Mark i. 4, 5.

And at the moment of humiliation, of voluntary identification with the sinfulness and hopelessness of his people, the answer was given. There could be no doubt of his "call"; no going back upon his renunciation; no alternative but to go through with the task laid upon him.

But the method was as yet undetermined. And the temptation to which the baptismal Spirit "drives" Jesus "forth" is probably rightly interpreted by S. Matthew and S. Luke, not simply as a reaction from the spiritual intensity of the Baptism, but as a time of self-scrutiny and self-determination with regard to the use of the divine powers which have been given to him. It is true that the primitive fact underlying the narratives—and it is one that must have rested on Jesus' own evidence—is simply that he was "tempted of Satan";[1] that the details of the temptation rest upon some other authority common to S. Matthew and to S. Luke; and that in this form, at any rate, the experience too much resembles a Scripture-quoting contest to be intended or taken as literally true. But in any case the position of the incident, and the stress laid upon it, justifies our regarding it as

[1] Mark i. 12, 13; Matt. iv. 1-11; Luke iv. 1-13.

Jesus' own explanation of the transition from a sudden "call" to a methodical ministry.

"Methodical" is perhaps too strong a word for the means and limits which Jesus prescribed to himself. His way of life, which, even more than his words or acts, won men's allegiance, and through the preaching and living of "the Way" converted the ancient world, included much that was purely spontaneous and personal. For our present purpose it may perhaps be divided into three parts: first, Jesus' way of teaching; secondly, his way of doing good; and thirdly, his way of living, which will include public and, so far as they do not trench on other divisions of our subject, private characteristics.

II

Jesus' favourite methods of teaching, so far as one is able to judge from the second gospel, were of five kinds. He would not have been conscious of the distinction between them. They were all spontaneous reactions to particular circumstances, the expressions of one mind and one way of speech to suit different cases. But, with this caution, we may reasonably give them separate consideration.

(i) The most primitive and effective kind of teaching is that which takes the form of a commentary upon acts. Jesus revealed God primarily through certain acts and a certain way of living: the preaching was always secondary. He did not argue with people: he made dogmatic statements, and offered no proof of them but personal authority, such as he manifested in his acts. One is commonly misled on this point by the disproportionate amount of pure *talking* in the other gospels: but S. Mark (and here the Acts entirely corroborates the second gospel) quite properly lays most stress on the acts of Jesus, and represents the teaching as growing naturally out of these. Further, such teaching most easily sticks in the memory, and is least liable to editorial alteration;[1] so that, whether or not we have in S. Mark's Gospel the recollections of S. Peter, we feel that in this class of sayings we get very near to the *ipsissima verba* of Jesus. Thus Jesus' claim to forgive sins is dependent upon the healing of a paralytic man;[2] the statement of his mission—" I came not to call the righteous, but sinners "—

[1] As a matter of fact, it is just in such sayings as these that the verbal identity of the three Gospels is most striking.
[2] Mark ii. 3-12.

arises out of an incident at a supper-party;[1] and the teaching about Sabbatarianism is the result of an incident in the course of a country walk.[2]

(ii) Another way of teaching characteristic of Jesus is that which proceeds by question and answer. S. Mark seems to be conscious that these sayings constitute a special class when he brings several of them together in one of his later chapters: he is perhaps also hinting that such formal questionings naturally occurred only towards the end of the ministry, when Jesus had become a recognised teacher, a power to be reckoned with. Thus Jesus' only political teaching is in answer to a question of the Pharisees and Herodians;[3] his argument for a future life is an appendix to an answer given to the Sadducees;[4] and it is the scribe's question, "What commandment is the first of all?" which introduces the Christian summary of the Decalogue.[5] Even the long apocalyptic discourse is represented as an answer to a private question by four disciples.[6]

(iii) It would be natural to expect that some at least of Jesus' teaching should consist of expositions of Scripture, especially of those parts of it which he had come to identify with the hopes

[1] Mark ii. 15-17.   [2] ii. 23-28.   [3] xii. 13-17.
[4] xii. 18-27.   [5] xii. 28-34.   [6] xiii. 3, 4.

and ideals of his own life. On three occasions, at any rate, he is represented as giving such teaching: and again S. Mark groups the incidents together. The parable of the vineyard culminates in a Messianic interpretation of the 118th Psalm;[1] the reality of life after death is proved by a verbal argument, which Jesus apparently gives as a discovery of his own, drawn from a passage in Exodus;[2] and an objection is urged against the current ideas of the Messiah from the words of Psalm cx.[3]

(iv) Many of the most striking sayings of Jesus are those which are expressed in proverbial or aphoristic forms. An aphorism is a little saying with a great meaning; its special force lies not so much in what it says as in what it suggests; it is often one-sided, and demands correction; or indeterminate, and demands individual interpretation. An aphorism need not be, and hardly claims to be, obviously true; but it reveals truth both in the speaker and in the hearer. "The sabbath was made for man, not man for the sabbath;"[4] "There is nothing hid, save that it should be manifested; neither was anything made secret, but that it should come to light;"[5] "With

---

[1] Mark xii. 10, 11.   [2] xii. 26, 27.
[3] xii. 35-37.   [4] ii. 27.   [5] iv. 22.

what measure ye mete, it shall be measured unto you;"¹ "He that hath, to him shall be given;"² "He that is not against us, is for us;"³ "Whosoever would save his life shall lose it"⁴—these are no more than a few of the sayings (the gospel is full of such) which have in an incomparable way summed up the old truth and inspired the new.

(v) But undoubtedly the most characteristic of all Jesus's ways of teaching, and the one that most nearly amounts to a method, is his use of metaphor and parable. The mere fact that such teaching would be more easily remembered than more abstract discourse is not enough to account for its actual bulk in the gospels: it is predominant there because it was Jesus' favourite way of speech.

Jesus did not always elaborate his parables. We have to distinguish, probably, between an earlier stage in his teaching, and a later. In the earlier, he was content with metaphorical sayings that hinted at rather than expressed a parable; the image of the strong man whom the robber must bind before he can spoil his house,⁵ or the comparison of the Kingdom of Heaven to the corn growing silently from seed-time to harvest,⁶

---

[1] Mark iv. 24.   [2] iv. 25.   [3] ix. 40.
[4] viii. 35.   [5] iii. 27.   [6] iv. 26-29.

might easily have been elaborated into fully expressed parables. The latter, indeed, may have been so treated by S. Matthew.[1] In the later stages of his ministry, or when a special audience or occasion demanded, Jesus used this method of teaching in the more complete form which we generally identify with the parable proper. Only two instances of this are given in the second gospel—the parable of the Sower,[2] and the parable of the Vineyard;[3] it is to S. Matthew and S. Luke that we go for the full development of this method.

S. Mark not merely supplies the groundwork for the more elaborate use of parables in the other gospels. He also records a discussion between Jesus and his disciples as to the intention of this method of teaching. The passage follows the parable of the Sower, and runs thus: "And when he was alone, they that were about him with the twelve, asked of him the parables. And he said unto them: Unto you is given the mystery of the Kingdom of God: but unto them that are without, all things are done in parables: that seeing they may see, and not per-

---

[1] Some critics hold that Matt. xiii. 24-30 (the parable of the Tares in the Field) is an elaboration of Mark iv. 26-29.
[2] Mark iv. 2-9.   [3] xii. 1-9.

JESUS' WAY OF LIFE

ceive; and hearing they may hear and not understand; lest haply they should turn again, and it should be forgiven them."[1] The first part of this explanation is what we should expect. A distinction is drawn between the plain instruction in "the mystery of the Kingdom of God" which is given to the disciples, and the veiled teaching which is given to those outside that body through parables. But the adaptation of Isaiah which follows is remarkable. "That seeing they may see" gives a purposive turn to the words, and credits Jesus with the intention of confirming the ignorant in their ignorance, the sinners in their sin, which we can hardly believe to have been in his mind. S. Matthew, feeling this difficulty, alters "*that*" to "*because*," but thereby loses the point of the quotation. Whatever the exact force given to the words in Jesus' original use, it is difficult not to think that they have been modified in the second gospel to suit the actual rejection of the Jews. Parables might be meant as a test of spiritual capacity: they could not be intended to hide the truth from any one with the capacity to discover it.

That this was the true aim of Jesus' parables is shown by S. Mark's own explanation with

[1] Mark iv. 10-12.

which the passage ends. "And with many such parables spake he the word unto them, as they were able to hear it: and without a parable spake he not unto them: but privately to his disciples he expounded all things."[1] "As they were able to hear it," exactly expresses the point: parables were intended to teach every individual just so much as he was able to learn, and no more.

III

The distinction which we have just noticed between the public and private teaching of Jesus is clearly marked in the narrative of the second gospel. S. Mark is generally very precise in stating to whom each part of the teaching was addressed. Thus, after answering a question by a group of Pharisees and Scribes, Jesus "called to him the multitude again," and spoke publicly the parable on the nature of defilement. "And when he was entered into the house from the multitude, his disciples asked of him the parable."[2] There are here three distinct audiences, and kinds of teaching. Or again, on the journey

---

[1] Mark iv. 33, 34; for an actual instance of this method *cf.* vii. 14-23.
[2] vii. 5-17.

to Cæsarea Philippi Jesus first questions his disciples as a whole, and foretells his passion. Then, the other disciples falling behind, S. Peter privately protests against his intention to die. " But he, turning about, and seeing his disciples, rebuked Peter, and saith, Get thee behind me, Satan "—that is, Peter is to fall back among the other disciples. And then, apparently as part of the same incident, "he called unto him the multitude with his disciples," and explained to them all the self-sacrifice involved in real discipleship.[1]

There were thus some parts of his teaching, especially those which could be thrown into the form of parables, which Jesus deliberately published: and there were others—summarily described as "the mystery of the Kingdom of God," which he only gave in private. If we ask of what the latter class of teachings consisted, it is not easy to give a very definite answer. Clearly, however, one great subject was, until quite the end of the ministry, guarded from general knowledge—Jesus' own claim to be the Messiah. It was not so much that Jesus dreaded the public enthusiasm and the political complications that such an avowal would at first involve: even

[1] Mark viii. 27-34.

more, perhaps, he felt the utter incongruity between the popular Messianic idea and his own self-consciousness, between the "Kingdom of our father David"[1] and the Kingdom of God. The Messianic conception was a hindrance to him, rather than a help: the public announcement of his claims could only lead ultimately, as, in fact, it did lead, to his rejection and death.

Consequently the first statement of Jesus' ministry,[2] the first questioning of the disciples' faith,[3] the predictions of the Passion,[4] the lessons of the Transfiguration,[5] and the teaching at the Last Supper,[6] are all addressed privately to a chosen body of followers. And most stress is laid, if we may judge from the position which this part of the teaching holds in the second gospel, upon the suffering and death through which alone the Christ can come into his Kingdom.

Another strain of the private teaching deals with the nature of Christian discipleship. The intimate relation between Jesus and his closest friends was not a thing to be discussed openly: his claim on their service, like his claim on their belief, could only gradually be revealed. Thus

---

[1] Mark xi. 10. [2] i. 38. [3] viii. 27-30.
[4] viii. 31; ix. 12, 31; x. 33.
[5] ix. 9-13. [6] xiv. 22-25.

it is to the disciples alone that Jesus explains the "mystery of the Kingdom of God," even when it lies no deeper than in the interpretation of a parable;[1] the first Christian "rule" is enjoined on the twelve apostles alone, for a special piece of work, not on all the disciples;[2] it is to his chosen followers that Jesus explains the special privilege of work done in his name,[3] or commands a charitable co-operation with those who are not disciples,[4] or blesses the complete renunciation of riches,[5] or teaches his favourite lesson on the virtue of humility.[6] Finally, the teaching about the nature of discipleship merges insensibly into spiritual lessons of a more general character, such as those on the true nature of defilement,[7] or on the need and power of faith.[8]

One can see from these instances that Jesus avoided the mistake, which great teachers have very commonly made, of thinking that he could always be understood; and that he was careful to speak in such a way that those who were listening to him could take what they were able to use, and yet not feel the loss of that which was beyond their apprehension. We do not

[1] Mark iv. 10-13, 33, 34.   [2] vi. 7-13.
[3] ix. 36, 37.   [4] ix. 38-41.   [5] x. 23-31.
[6] x. 42-45.   [7] vii. 17-23.   [8] xi. 22-25.

wonder at the characteristic refrain with which the Evangelists have closed so many of the parables, "Who hath ears to hear, let him hear."[1]

IV

If it be true that Jesus revealed God primarily by his way of living, we shall expect to learn much from a consideration of his method of doing good. Here, again, "method" is too strong a word. Jesus' acts of goodness were nothing if not spontaneous. If they seem to illustrate a principle or to conform to a rule, it is because they are the natural expressions of a single character which was a law to itself. But, with this reservation, one can profitably raise the question, What was the aim and character of Jesus' chief acts of goodness—his miracles of healing?

First, then, Jesus did not work miracles in order to make himself known, or to bring people to his preaching. This is what we should already expect from his attitude towards the popular Messianic beliefs. It is entirely borne out by the precautions which he takes to work special miracles in private, and to secure the silence of those whom he has cured. Thus the raising of

[1] Mark iv. 9, etc.

JESUS' WAY OF LIFE

Jairus's daughter (the only miracle of its kind in the second gospel) is done in the presence of the girl's parents and three chosen disciples;[1] in the instance of a deaf man with an impediment in his speech—a specially difficult case to cure—"he took him aside from the multitude privately" before doing anything for him;[2] in another similar case "he took hold of the blind man by the hand, and brought him out of the village";[3] and it was not till "Jesus saw that a multitude came running together" that he cast out the dumb and deaf spirit from the boy at the foot of the Mount of Transfiguration.[4]

To secure the silence of those whom he has cured, Jesus frequently forbids the evil spirits who recognise him to make him known.[5] In the case of a leper he is particularly insistent—"he strictly charged him, and straightway sent him out, and saith unto him, See thou say nothing to any man."[6] Jairus and his wife he "charged ... much that no man should know" of the raising of their daughter.[7] Of the first of the two special cases of healing which S. Mark alone mentions it is recorded that "he charged them that

---

[1] Mark v. 37, 40.   [2] vii. 33.   [3] viii. 23.
[4] ix. 25.   [5] i. 25, 34; iii. 12.
[6] i. 43, 44.   [7] v. 43.

they should tell no man,"[1] and of the second that "he sent him away to his home, saying, Do not even enter into the village".[2]

The one possible exception to this general practice is the case of the Gerasene demoniac, whom Jesus will not allow to follow him as a disciple, "but saith unto him, Go to thy house unto thy friends, and tell them how great things the Lord hath done for thee, and how he had mercy on thee".[3] But considering that it is to his family and friends, not to the world at large, that the man is to bear witness, and that this event happened in Peræa, which Jesus himself did not intend to evangelise, and where the ordinary reasons against publicity did not exist, one is probably justified in regarding this incident as "the exception which proves the rule".

Secondly, if Jesus did not work miracles in order to obtain publicity, neither did he do so in order to prove his personal claims. There is probably only one case in the second gospel of which this might be alleged—the healing of a paralytic man at Capernaum as a proof of the claim to forgive sins—"But that ye may know that the Son of man hath power on earth to forgive sins, (he saith to the sick of the palsy,) I say

[1] Mark vii. 36.   [2] viii. 26   [3] v. 19.

JESUS' WAY OF LIFE

unto thee, Arise".[1] This incident stands quite alone in the Gospel, and cannot safely be taken as representing Jesus' general practice. Judging from the number of miracles that have no evidential purpose, it is more probable that this instance is exceptional, and that our general statement holds good.

What, then, was Jesus' general aim in working miracles? We shall hardly be wrong if we accept provisionally the most natural explanation, namely that he did these good acts spontaneously, and as part of the work of God which he had been sent to do, without any ulterior object or conscious policy. As S. Peter put it, he "went about doing good, and healing all that were oppressed of the devil; for God was with him".[2] No theory could be more true or more worthy than that simple statement.

Something should be added as to the *nature* of the miracles, so far as it affects Jesus' method of doing good. For instance, what amount of truth is there in the idea that Jesus demanded faith on the part of those whom he healed? If he did so, it is a point that considerably affects his method. Certainly he was unable to do any "mighty work" at Nazareth because of the

[1] Mark ii. 10. [2] Acts x. 38.

unbelief of the people.¹ It was the faith of the palsied man's friends (and, it is implied, of the man himself) which prompted the words of forgiveness.² Both to the woman with the issue of blood, and to the blind man, Bartimæus, he said, "thy faith hath made thee whole".³ In the case of a boy with a dumb spirit Jesus seems to wish for, and to aim at drawing out some expression of the father's faith.⁴ These are certainly some instances in which Jesus connects faith with healing; but it is never stated as a necessary condition of it.

And, indeed, in the great majority of the miracles described by S. Mark, nothing is said as to the need of faith, and we are not led to suppose that Jesus required it. The persons chosen to receive these benefits are men casually met in the synagogue or the country-side,⁵ a sick woman in the house of a friend,⁶ or the indiscriminate sufferers in the village or the crowd.⁷ If we ask what prompted Jesus' action in such cases, the answer again seems to be the most natural one. He worked miracles because he

[1] Mark vi. 5, 6: it is implied that the hindrance was lack of faith.
[2] ii. 5. [3] v. 34; x. 52. [4] ix. 23, 24.
[5] i. 23; v. 2. [6] i. 30. [7] iii. 10-11; vi. 56.

JESUS' WAY OF LIFE 59

was asked to do so: or he healed people because he was sorry for them. Jairus's urgent prayer for his daughter, or the request of a blind man's friends (as on two occasions) are the only reasons given for some of the most difficult miracles.[1] In two cases—the healing of a leper, and the second miracle of feeding—compassion is clearly stated as the motive for the miracle;[2] and this seems to be implied also in the feeding of the five thousand, and in the walking on the lake.[3]

There remains one class of miraculous healing which is of rather different kind. In the case of the woman with an issue of blood who touched Jesus in the crowd, the cure was worked by the mere act of contact, and by the woman's faith. The healing power is conceived as something almost material: Jesus perceived "that the power proceeding from him had gone forth," without any will of his own.[4] Nor was this an exceptional case, if one may judge from S. Mark's summary of the ministry of healing in Galilee—" Wheresoever he entered, into villages, or into cities, or into the country, they laid the sick in the market-places, and besought him that they

[1] Mark v. 22, 23; vii. 32; viii. 22.
[2] i. 41; viii. 2.   [3] vi. 37, 48.   [4] v. 30.

might touch if it were but the border of his garment: and as many as touched him were made whole."[1] Whatever may have been the exact nature of the influence so exercised, it is clear that at this point the idea of "method" finally breaks down. Jesus' power to heal, at all times liberal and spontaneous, easily called out by pity or request—lying, as one might say, very near the surface of his personality—sometimes passed beyond his control, so that he could not help working miracles. Here the discussion passes outside its present point. Enough has been said to show that the truest account of Jesus' way of doing good will be that which is most natural, and that Jesus was most methodical when he was most himself.

V

The third head under which one may consider Jesus' way of life is his method of living. The main features of this were, no doubt, largely determined by influences which are rather presupposed than expressed in the gospels—the social standard and ideals under which Jesus had been brought up, or the traditional way of life of the

[1] Mark vi. 56.

JESUS' WAY OF LIFE

Jewish prophets, or the practical necessities of the ministry. The strongest evidence, at any rate in the case of the second gospel, consists of quite incidental references to minor points and characteristics. But before passing on to these, attention must be called to S. Mark's general representation of the early ministry. It is described repeatedly as a busy, hurried, crowded life, in which almost every hour was lived in public, and there was no leisure from the constant demands for teaching or for help. S. Mark's constant use of "straightway," by which one incident follows upon another in breathless hurry, is not merely a trick of style, but also a record of fact.[1] At Capernaum, where Jesus was staying in S. Peter's house, "all the city was gathered together at the door," and he could only find leisure for prayer by getting up before dawn and going into a desert place outside the city.[2] Soon afterwards, in consequence of the healing of a leper, who (in spite of Jesus' prohibition) "spread abroad the matter," he "could no more openly enter into a city, but was without in desert places; and they came to him

---

[1] *e.g.*, Mark i. 10, 12, 18, 20, 21, 23, 29, 30.
[2] i. 33-35.

from every quarter".[1] During a later visit to Capernaum, when Jesus was again staying, apparently, with S. Peter, the house was so full of people that "there was no longer room for them, no, not even about the door"; and the friends of a paralytic who wished to be healed, "when they could not come nigh unto him for the crowd, . . . uncovered the roof where he was: and when they had broken it up, they let down the bed whereon the sick of the palsy lay".[2] At meal-times the room would be full of publicans and sinners: "for there were many, and they followed him":[3] once it is recorded that "the multitude cometh together again, so that they could not so much as eat bread";[4] and once that "there were many coming and going, and they had no leisure so much as to eat".[5] Jesus' own relatives cannot reach him, but are forced to send a message through the crowd:[6] the multitude so throngs him when he goes to Jairus's house that the disciples think it absurd to ask, "Who touched me?"[7] Sometimes Jesus was forced to escape from the crowds, and to secure a little quiet by taking boat across the lake of

---

[1] Mark i. 45. [2] ii. 1-4. [3] ii. 15. [4] iii. 20.
[5] vi. 31. [6] iii. 31, 32. [7] v. 31.

Galilee.¹ Later, he had to go farther afield, but was still unsuccessful in escaping the publicity which had come to be such a burden—"And from thence he arose, and went away into the borders of Tyre and Sidon. And he entered into a house, and would have no man know it: and he could not be hid."² The journey "into the villages of Cæsarea Philippi" was almost certainly undertaken for the same reason.³ But even this seclusion was only possible for a time; and though, when he came back into Galilee, he "passed through" as secretly as possible, and "would not that any man should know it,"⁴ yet soon afterwards the "multitudes come together unto him again":⁵ a "great multitude" follows him out of Jericho,⁶ and crowds go before and follow after as he enters into Jerusalem.⁷

Putting aside the central part of the ministry, during which he seems almost to have been in hiding from the enthusiasm of the people, it would be difficult to exaggerate the crowd and stress of Jesus' short public life. These conditions were forced upon him; they were not

---

¹ Mark iv. 35; vi. 45; viii. 10, 13 (on the first occasion he even went by night, and in risk of stormy weather).
² vii. 24.   ³ viii. 27.   ⁴ ix. 30.
⁵ x. 1.   ⁶ x. 46.   ⁷ xi. 8, 9.

of his own choosing. The wonderful thing is that the life and teaching in themselves bear none of the marks of hurry or distress, but are calm, spacious, and simple to an amazing degree.

VI

Among such scenes and circumstances Jesus moved, leaving everywhere certain impressions of himself, by word or act or look, upon those with whom he dealt. His method was to be himself. Can we recapture those impressions? Not directly, nor in detail. But the second Gospel is full of hints and clues from which it is quite possible to reconstruct some of the external characteristics, at any rate, of Jesus' personality.

He was known as one who could easily be moved to pity. "Moved with compassion," he healed a leper, and fed a multitude;[1] on another occasion "he came forth and saw a great multitude, and he had compassion on them, because they were as sheep not having a shepherd: and he began to teach them many things".[2]

He could feel sympathy for his friends in a time of danger,[3] and love a young man at first sight.[4] He was full of little acts of friendliness,

[1] Mark i. 41; viii. 2.   [2] vi. 34.   [3] vi. 48.   [4] x. 21.

JESUS' WAY OF LIFE

calling a palsied man "Child,"[1] taking a blind man by the hand,[2] and holding a child in his arms;[3] and once, when the people brought their little children to him, he "took them in his arms, and blessed them, laying his hands upon them".[4]

But he was known, too, as one who could be angry with just cause. He "looked round about on them with anger, being grieved at the hardening of their heart":[5] "he sighed deeply in his spirit" when the Pharisees asked for a sign:[6] "O faithless generation," he cries (apparently) to the disciples, "how long shall I be with you? how long shall I bear with you?"[7] witnessing to a disappointment of which he must often have been conscious, but which he generally suppressed. Once, too, he expresses surprise,[8] and once appreciation of a clever retort.[9]

These notices are not very numerous. But their cumulative effect is to show that Jesus was by no means always the quiet, unemotional person that one sometimes imagines him to have been. Rather, he gave full value to feeling as

---

[1] Mark ii. 5 (τέκνον). [2] viii. 23. [3] ix. 36.
[4] x. 16. [5] iii. 5. [6] viii. 12.
[7] ix. 19. [8] vi. 6. [9] vii. 28, 29.

a guide to conduct, and his emotions moved strongly not far below the surface.

Among characteristic acts, which S. Mark notices, the kindly treatment of blind men and children has already been mentioned. But the one that appears most often, and seems to have been most vividly impressed on the memory of S. Mark's informant, is something in Jesus' way of *looking*. He would "look round about on" those with whom he was talking, either in anger,[1] or in love,[2] or in inquiry,[3] or in warning:[4] he looked "up to heaven" in the attitude of prayer, at the miraculous breaking of bread,[5] and at the cure of a deaf man:[6] and of the young ruler it is recorded that "Jesus looking upon him loved him".[7] The interest of these things is not that S. Mark's informant should have noticed them, but that he should have been unable not to notice them. They were almost certainly characteristics of Jesus that inevitably reappear in the narrative, not by design, but by its unconscious truth to facts.

The same kind of result follows with regard to Jesus' characteristic words. S. Mark on four occasions records in the original Aramaic the

[1] Mark iii. 5. [2] iii. 34. [3] v. 32. [4] x. 23.
[5] vi. 41. [6] vii. 34. [7] x. 21.

ipsissima verba of which it often seems so hard to be certain—"Talitha cumi" at the raising of Jairus's daughter,[1] "Ephphatha" at the opening of a blind man's eyes,[2] "Abba, Father" at Gethsemane,[3] and "Eloi, Eloi, lama sabachthani" upon the cross.[4] In addition, two characteristic refrains, at least, are recorded—"Who hath ears to hear, let him hear,"[5] and the emphatic "Verily I say unto you".[6] Even the smallest indications of this nature help to bring one within sight and sound of the Jesus whom the disciples knew so well that they have not left behind a single clear indication of his personal appearance.

VII

Upon one point the scattered hints that we are considering become more coherent. Constantly living and travelling with Jesus, the disciples would first come to observe and then to take for granted the informal rules of their common life. It would never occur to them to describe in what order they journeyed, or at what times and in what ways Jesus spoke to them.

---

[1] Mark v. 41. [2] vii. 34. [3] xiv. 36.
[4] xv. 34. [5] iv. 9. [6] iii. 28; x. 15, 29.

Yet it is in hints of just these things that the second gospel is, quite unconsciously, so rich.

We gather, for instance, that on a journey various practices held. Sometimes Jesus walks apart from the disciples—this seems to be the most general rule—but near enough to be aware of the nature of their conversation.[1] On the journey to Cæsarea Philippi he walks with them, questioning them and teaching them: but this is only for a short time; later, the disciples fall behind, except the one who has something special to say to him; later again, we find him calling "the multitude with the disciples," to give them the final lesson arising out of the day's talk.[2] If this evidence be thought precarious, it may be compared with the very similar case during the journey to Jerusalem. On this occasion "Jesus was going before" the disciples, and "they that followed were afraid"—the followers in this case seem to have included others besides the twelve. Jesus then takes the twelve (probably calling them to walk with him) and explains to them the object of the journey. They then fall behind. Later, two of them, James and John, catch him up to ask a special favour of him. Rebuked, they fall back again, and tell the other ten what

[1] Mark ix. 33, 34. [2] viii. 27-34.

JESUS' WAY OF LIFE

has passed. Finally, Jesus calls them all to him for the second time, and teaches the lesson of humility to which the incident points.[1] If, as seems to be the case, this is all one scene, it gives an unstudied but very vivid picture of what was probably a common practice in Jesus' relations with his disciples.

The Master's separateness from his disciples is noticed also on other occasions. During the storm on the lake he sleeps apart "in the stern ... on the cushion";[2] during a voyage by day the disciples dispute apart:[3] Jesus works his hardest miracles away from them,[4] or admits only the chosen three:[5] and he leaves them when he wishes to pray,[6] though the three may be with him on the Mountain of Transfiguration,[7] and not far away in the Garden of Gethsemane.[8] Again, when he wishes to speak to the disciples Jesus generally calls them to him.[9] Sometimes he sits among them to teach them:[10] it

---

[1] Mark x. 32-42.

[2] iv. 38 (but *cf.* the possible literary dependence of this passage, p. 119).

[3] viii. 16, 17.

[4] vii. 33 ; viii. 23 (probably to be so interpreted).

[5] v. 37.   [6] i. 35 ; vi. 46.   [7] ix. 2.

[8] xiv. 33, 34.   [9] viii. 1 ; ix. 35 ; xii. 43.   [10] ix. 35, 36.

was when he "sat down over against the treasury" that he saw the poor widow cast in her two mites;[1] and it was "as he sat on the Mount of Olives over against the temple" that four of the disciples asked the question which introduced the apocalyptic discourse.[2]

Thus, though he could call them "children,"[3] Jesus was not inclined to be very familiar with the disciples. True humility was in no sense inconsistent with "keeping his distance," and accepting the unquestioned supremacy which was accorded to him.

VIII

One turns from the attempt to inquire into Jesus' way of life with at any rate one strong impression—that he was a real person, and that he can and should be studied as such. This is a truism, but an important one. It is very easy to think that we know who Jesus was and how he lived: but our account, when we are driven to it, is too often vague, inconsistent and second-hand. To have made an attempt, on however small a scale, to draw plain conclusions from the best evidence is to realise how

---

[1] Mark xii. 41, 42.   [2] xiii. 3.   [3] x. 24.

much remains to be learnt about the nature of the Incarnation. The dogmatic and devotional development of Christianity will always be halting and unsatisfactory, unless there is corresponding to it a sincere and thorough attempt to reconstruct the figure of the historical Jesus.

CHAPTER IV

JESUS' MIND

I

FEW questions are more difficult to understand or to discuss than that which now claims consideration. Not merely the nature of Jesus' authority as a teacher, but one whole aspect of the Incarnation, is here under discussion. And yet it may be held that the method which we have laid down for our inquiry will enable us to disregard most of the theological entanglements which the controversies of centuries have raised around the essential question—What was the nature of Jesus' mind? For perhaps the greater part of these controversies has been due, not to any attempt to account for the facts as they appear in the gospels, but to a desire to be consistent with certain theological or philosophical presuppositions: whereas the sole endeavour of the *a posteriori* method is to find out what are the facts, and to frame a hypothesis that will fit them. Whether enough data are discoverable, and whether an adequate hypothesis can be built on them, remains to be seen : the attempt is at any rate worth making, and the method a sound one.

The subject falls naturally into two parts. The first concerns the matter, the second the manner of thought. We shall first try to gauge, from the evidence of the second gospel, the extent and the limitations of Jesus' knowledge : we shall then try to find indications of his more habitual ways of thinking—the nature and workings of his mind.

II

We shall have learnt by this time that no account of Jesus can be adequate which fails to reckon with the influences of his childhood and youth. It is true, they do not so much concern the nature as the content of his thought ; but with regard to the latter, at any rate, they cannot be ignored.

Summarily, we should say that on most subjects Jesus shared the knowledge and the ignorance of his neighbours. The evidence for this is inferential, and is drawn more from what

S. Mark does not, than from what he does state. There are great tracts of human interest which seem to be untouched by Jesus' intelligence. History, literature, science, politics, art—he neither cares for these things, nor is he conscious that he might care for them. Of course one soon learns to take this for granted. But the reason why one does so is not often explicitly stated. It is simply because Jesus was a Jew, and a Galilean, and a carpenter. The silence of the gospels on these big subjects is not to be explained in any other way. It is arbitrary to suppose that Jesus *could* have dealt with these things, but had no need to; or that he accommodated himself to the point of view of those among whom he lived. Again, it is true that to him the things of God were all in all: but we cannot suppose that he would deliberately limit his knowledge or suppress his reason in the interests of religion. And again, the gospels are at best fragmentary records, and contain only a few of Jesus' sayings: are we justified, it may be said, in judging from them? The answer is that, unless the fragments are representative, and no essential element in Jesus' character is unrecorded there, we shall be unable to arrive at any safe conclusions, whether in this or in other matters. It might be necessary to adopt this sceptical view, but the evidence, on the whole, is against it. If, then, the gospels are representative, it follows that when they leave Jesus silent upon these big subjects it is because he was silent: nor can any explanation of this be preferred to the most natural one—that Jesus shared the knowledge and the ignorance of his neighbours.

III

The normal content of Jesus' mind, then, on ordinary subjects, was such as one would expect in a Galilean countryman early in the first century A.D. That is the principal conclusion that one draws from the general impression given by the second gospel. One has yet to examine it more in detail, and to work out the particular data for Jesus' social, moral and religious outlook. And one has to give weight to those other subjects in which Jesus' knowledge and insight was undoubtedly quite abnormal.

The second of these points may be taken first. There **are** several important respects in which, according to evidence which one can hardly dispute, Jesus' mind was not normal—though those who admit this would probably differ as to the degree of abnormality required.

The most obvious of these matters is the sureness and authoritativeness of Jesus' teaching about the essential things of religion—about the nature of God in relation to man, and of man in relation to God. From the very beginning of his ministry "they were astonished at his teaching: for he taught them as one having authority, and not as the scribes".[1] "And they were all amazed, insomuch that they questioned among themselves, saying, What is this? A new teaching!"[2] Again, at Nazareth, "many hearing him were astonished, saying, Whence hath this man these things? and, What is the wisdom that is given unto this man . . . ?"[3] It never seems to occur to Jesus that he may be ignorant, or wrong, in dealing with religious questions. There is no trace in his teaching of S. Paul's distinction between revelation and opinion; we cannot imagine him saying: "Concerning this or that matter I have no commandment of God; but I give my judgment, as one that hath obtained mercy of God to be faithful"; or, "This is the better course, after my judg-

---

[1] Mark i. 22.   [2] i. 27.   [3] vi. 2.

ment: and I think that I also have the Spirit of God".[1] On the contrary, he speaks of God with the simplicity of a child, the sureness of an expert, and the insight of a saint: and he does it without effort, or immaturity, or self-consciousness. All this, certainly, must be taken into account in any attempt to understand the nature of the Incarnation.

Again, Jesus has in an abnormal degree that power of insight into men's hearts and minds which belongs to some extent to all spiritually minded people. Such at least seems to be implied when S. Mark describes him as "perceiving in his spirit that they [the Scribes] so reasoned within themselves,"[2] or as "knowing their hypocrisy,"[3] when the Pharisees and Herodians asked the question about the Imperial Tribute. But certainly little is made of this in the second gospel, compared with its much greater prominence in the other evangelists: in the fourth gospel, indeed, it is raised almost to the level of a dogma, and is constantly emphasized.

More noticeable than the last, perhaps, is Jesus' power of prophecy or presentiment. Quite early in his ministry he foresaw the time of

[1] 1 Cor. vii. 25, 40.   [2] Mark ii. 8.
[3] xii. 15.

separation from his disciples—"the days will come, when the bridegroom shall be taken away from them".[1] "O faithless generation," he exclaimed (apparently) to the disciples, "how long shall I be with you? how long shall I bear with you?"[2] The apostles who wished to share his glory he reminded of the coming Passion—"Are ye able to drink the cup that I drink? or to be baptized with the baptism that I am baptized with?"[3] Of the woman who anointed him in Simon's house he is reported to have said: "Wheresoever the Gospel shall be preached throughout the whole world, that also which this woman hath done shall be spoken of for a memorial of her".[4] And S. Peter's assertion of faithfulness was met with the prophecy—"Verily I say unto thee, that thou to-day, even this night, before the cock crow twice, shalt deny me thrice".[5]

The force of this evidence lies chiefly in the unimportance of the things foretold, and the unlikelihood that such presentiments would be inserted in the light of later events. For this reason less certainty can be felt with regard to the genuineness—at least in some of their details—of the repeated prophecies of the Passion and

[1] Mark ii. 20. [2] ix. 19. [3] x. 38.
[4] xiv. 9; cf. xiii. 10. [5] xiv. 30.

Resurrection.[1] Undoubtedly Jesus did foresee his end: but the outline of the original prediction has probably been filled in—as was almost inevitable—from a knowledge of the actual events of the Death and Resurrection. The same criticism applies to the other great class of Jesus' personal presentiments—those dealing with his second coming, so far as genuinely eschatological ideas have become modified by contact with the actual events attending the fall of Jerusalem. But in any case, when due allowance has been made for such influences, we are faced with the fact that Jesus foretold for himself a return "in the glory of his Father with the holy angels,"[2] and imagined himself as "the Son of man coming in clouds with great power and glory,"[3] to set up the Kingdom of God in the world. We shall have more to say about these and similar passages shortly: for the present one must notice that these sayings of Jesus, regarded as prophecies, and taken in the sense in which the Church understood him to have made them, *viz.*, as referring to a speedy return within the lifetime of the first disciples,

[1] Mark viii. 31; ix. 12, 31; x. 33, 34 (the criticism applies particularly to this last passage). *cf.* p. 246.
[2] viii. 38. [3] xiii. 26.

never came true. Whatever be said of this, it can hardly be regarded as anything but a serious difficulty. Just as the whole basis of Jesus' religious life—his faith in the presence and love of God—seems to be challenged by the cry of despair on the cross, so his intellectual groundwork would be threatened, if the chief hope that filled his mind and inspired his life proved false. The explanation is probably to be looked for in the inadequacy of the Messianic idea (including the language of Daniel with regard to the second coming) to express the real meaning of Jesus' presentiment. He used the popular language about himself, because nothing better was available. He knew that it did not satisfy him. And that perhaps is why, after the narrower prediction, "This generation shall not pass away until all these things be accomplished," there follows the wider and truer idea, "Heaven and earth shall pass away: but my words shall not pass away".[1]

IV

It will be convenient at this point to illustrate both the matter and manner of Jesus' thoughts

---

[1] Mark xiii. 30, 31.

by dealing more in detail with three important questions—his treatment of Scripture, his demonology, or attitude towards the powers of evil, and his eschatology. It will then only remain to draw what inferences one may from Jesus' methods of teaching—already in part discussed—as to his methods of thinking.

(i) It would probably be difficult to exaggerate the influence of the Old Testament Scriptures upon Jesus' ideas and ways of thought. The actual quotations from or references to these Scriptures which may be traced in S. Mark's report of his sayings hardly represent the full extent of their influence. But they are probably, so far as they go, representative ; and one may safely draw from them certain conclusions as to Jesus' use of the Old Testament.

Jesus' quotations from or references to the Old Testament in the second gospel may be tabulated thus :—

Book of O.T.	Subject of Quotation.	Reference.
Genesis i. 27, ii. 24	On the permanence of marriage	x. 6-8.
,, xviii. 14	"All things are possible with God"	x. 27.
,, xix. 26	Returning back to take a cloke	xiii. 16.
Exodus xx. 12, xxi. 17	Honouring father and mother	vii. 10.
,, xx. 12	The Decalogue	x. 19.
,, iii. 6	Moses and the bush, a proof of future life	xii. 26.
,, xxiv. 8	The blood of the covenant	xiv. 24.
Leviticus xiii. 49	Priest and leper	i. 44.
,, xix. 18	Law of love	xii. 31.
Deuteronomy vi. 4, 5	Summary of the Decalogue	xii. 29, 30.
,, xiii. 1-3	False prophets	xiii. 22.
,, xxx. 4	The gathering of the elect	xiii. 27.
1 Samuel xxi. 6	David and the shew-bread	ii. 26.
Job xlii. 2	"All things are possible with God"	x. 27.
Psalms cxviii. 22, 23	The stone rejected by the builders	xii. 10, 11.
,, cx. 1	David and the Son of David	xii. 36.
,, xxii. 1	Last words on the Cross	xv. 34.
Isaiah vi. 9, 10	Reason for using parables	iv. 12.
,, xxix. 13	Hypocrisy of scribes and Pharisees	vii. 6, 7.

Book of O.T.	Subject of Quotation.	Reference.
Isaiah lxvi. 24	"Their worm dieth not"	ix. 48.
,, lvi. 7	The temple a house of prayer	xi. 17.
,, v. 1	Parable of the Vineyard	xii. 1.
,, xiii. 10, xxxiv. 4	Eschatological language	xiii. 24.
Jeremiah vii. 11	"A den of robbers"	xi. 17.
Ezekiel xvii. 23	Mustard tree	iv. 32.
Daniel iv. 12, 21	Mustard tree	iv. 32.
,, ii. 28	"These things must needs come to pass"	xiii. 7.
,, ix. 27, xii. 11	"The abomination of desolation"	xiii. 14.
,, xii. 1	Tribulation	xiii. 19.
,, vii. 13	"The Son of man coming in clouds"	xiii. 26, xiv. 62.
Joel iii. 13	The reaping of the harvest	iv. 29.
Micah vii. 6	"Children shall rise up against parents"	xiii. 12.
Zechariah viii. 6	"All things are possible with God"	x. 27.
,, ii. 6	The gathering of the elect	xiii. 27.
,, xiii. 7	"I will smite the shepherd"	xiv. 27.
Malachi iv. 5	The coming of Elijah	ix. 12.

When we consider this list in detail, several interesting points emerge. Thus, Jesus shows a distinct preference for the legislative, devotional, and prophetic books, as compared with the historical. He does not [1] derive moral lessons, as one might expect him to do, from the patriarchs and heroes of his people. He does not draw out the analogy between himself and the great prophets, such as Elijah. His interest in the Scriptures is subjective, not objective, meditative, not scientific.

Again, it would not be very hazardous to conjecture that Jesus' favourite books—those that spoke to him most vividly of his own life and death and hopes beyond death—were the Psalter, Isaiah, Daniel, and perhaps Exodus. It cannot be an accident that the form of Jesus' "call," repeated at the Baptism and the Transfiguration, came from Isaiah, or that the words of a Psalm were on his lips when he died. These books were a constant source to him both of language and of ideas: and one may perhaps judge from the greater frequency of such quotations in the later part of the gospel that Jesus increasingly identified himself with the Messianic language of the Old Testament.

---

[1] With the exception of ii. 26.

(ii) Jesus' ideas as to the authorship of the books of the Old Testament were those usual among his contemporaries. The Mosaic authorship of the Pentateuch seems to be taken for granted. It is separately assumed in the case of Genesis,[1] and of Exodus—the latter on two occasions.[2] The Psalms as a whole are probably attributed to David, and an important argument is based upon the Davidic authorship of Psalm cx.[3] In these cases it is arbitrary to go outside the natural explanation, and to suppose that Jesus accepted contemporary ideas, knowing them to be wrong. It was simply that he shared the ignorance as well as the knowledge of his neighbours in such matters.

(iii) Jesus, like his contemporaries, regarded the appeal to Scripture as authoritative. Two instances may be given of this attitude. The point of his answer to the Pharisees' question about the lawfulness of divorce is, not that he supersedes the Law with the Gospel, but that he goes behind the Mosaic compromise to the original and real meaning of the Law. His intention is to interpret, not to legislate. And the ground upon which he bases his reading of the Law is the literal interpretation of certain words

[1] Mark x. 3.   [2] vii. 10, xii. 26.   [3] xii. 36.

in Genesis which are taken as an authoritative and divine command.[1]

Again, the pedantic and rather frivolous question put by the Sadducees is met by Jesus with a double answer, both parts of which rely upon the appeal to scriptural authority. First, he says that if the Sadducees had known "the Scriptures" and "the power of God" they would not have fallen into such an error as to suppose that marriage could have any meaning in the resurrection life—though he does not say to what particular Scriptures he is referring. Secondly, he points out a proof of the reality of life after death—the denial of which was the real ground of the Sadducees' difficulty—in God's words to Moses, "I am the God of Abraham, and the God of Isaac, and the God of Jacob".[2] This, apparently, was not a "stock argument" for the future life, but a piece of private exegesis. Yet its force rests upon a literal, if not a forced interpretation of an isolated text—a fact which throws some light upon the manner of Jesus' use of the Old Testament, as well as upon the authority which he attached to it.

(iv) Jesus found the clue to the Old Testament in himself. This is probably the most

[1] Mark x. 2-9.   [2] xii. 18-27.

important point to remember under the present head. It was the discovery that John the Baptist fulfilled the scriptural forecasts of the Forerunner which first made Jesus conscious of his own Messiahship. From the day when his "call" came in the words of Isaiah,[1] the whole language of the Old Testament took on a new meaning for him. God's will—the Kingdom of God, and God's hope—the promise of a Messiah, seemed to be working themselves out in him. The Transfiguration objectifies this idea: Moses, representing the Law, and Elijah, representing the Prophets, are seen "talking with Jesus";[2] and S. Luke is probably supplying the obvious inference when he says that they "spake of the decease which he was about to accomplish at Jerusalem".[3] This was the idea that more and more obsessed Jesus' mind during the latter part of his ministry. Two other instances may be given—the interpretation of the Messianic Psalm cx. as applying to himself,[4] and the similar use made of Psalm cxvii. as the conclusion of a passage in which Jesus adapts to his own circumstances a parable from Isaiah.[5]

(v) It only remains to notice Jesus' method

[1] Mark i. 11 [2] ix. 4. [3] Luke ix. 31.
[4] Mark xii. 35-37. [5] xii. 10, 11.

of interpreting the Scriptures. One example of this has already been touched on—the derivation of an argument for the future life from a verse in Exodus; but at least one other good instance may be mentioned in the exegesis of the 110th Psalm.[1] Here the whole force of the argument turns upon the assumption that the psalm was written by David, that he was inspired ("in the Holy Spirit") when he wrote it, and that it was of prophecy of the coming Messiah. That is to say, Jesus' use of the psalm presupposes a particular theory of inspiration, and a particular authorship, which, to say no more, are not generally accepted as right.

We conclude, then, that what was new and unique in Jesus' treatment of Scripture was the sureness with which he appropriated it to his own spiritual experience; and that what was conventional and inadequate was the secular knowledge and method of interpretation through which he tried to explain that sureness. Here again, as in other matters already mentioned, one feels that Jesus himself—his faith and hope and personal consciousness—were something far greater than could be expressed by the only

[1] xii. 35-37.

ideas and forms that were available for him, or intelligible to his contemporaries. The Gospel of the Incarnation is a Gospel of limitations.

V

In dealing with Jesus' demonology, or the nature of his beliefs as to what are commonly called the powers of evil, three questions seem to need an answer. What was Jesus' belief as to demonic "possession"? What was the nature of his "understanding" with evil spirits? and what power had he over them?

(i) It is impossible, on any sound critical theory, to separate the miraculous parts of the second gospel from the non-miraculous. And of the former so large a proportion consists of contests between Jesus and "evil spirits," and these are described so naïvely and naturally, that one cannot doubt that such events, whatever their exact meaning, played a large part in the every-day life of Jesus and his disciples. The further question must then be raised, whether S. Mark's unquestioning acceptance of the theory of "possession" represents the normal view of Jesus and his contemporaries, or the later judgment of a member of a Church in which special powers of healing were a matter of faith and practice. Almost certainly, from the acquiescence of the common people in Jesus' attitude, it represents the former. Jesus was not a clairvoyant, with a special power of visualising the causes of disease. He moved among a people who habitually regarded certain diseases as due to the indwelling of personal powers of evil, and he shared their opinion. But if, whilst sharing it, he was able to cure the diseases, it does not follow that the opinion was right.

Did Jesus, then, believe in the existence of a personal power of evil? Almost certainly he did. On his own authority it is recorded that "He was in the wilderness forty days, tempted of Satan"[1]—though it must be noticed that it is S. Matthew and S. Luke who add those details which make Satan definitely a person, and that S. Luke alone introduces the extraordinary theory that all the world is in the power of the Evil One.[2] In the parable of the sower he pictures Satan as a bird which comes and takes away the seed of the Gospel from men's hearts.[3] S. Peter is regarded as in some way possessed by Satan when he tempts Jesus not to suffer and

[1] Mark i. 13.
[2] Matt. iv. 1-11; Luke iv. 1-13, especially iv. 6.
[3] Mark iv. 15.

JESUS' MIND

die; and is therefore rebuked in very similar words to those used (according to S. Matthew) at the Temptation—"Get thee behind me Satan".[1] (In the same spirit S. Luke reports that "Satan entered into Judas,"[2] and makes Jesus say to S. Peter, on a later occasion, "Satan asked to have you".[3]) Or again, "How can Satan cast out Satan? . . . If Satan is risen up against himself, he cannot stand:"[4] and the point is enforced by the parable of the strong man (Satan) whom Jesus binds and spoils.[5]

(ii) That Jesus believed in the reality of a personal spirit of evil is rendered more likely by the "understanding" which clearly existed between him and the "evil spirits" which he cast out. At the time of Jesus' first visit to the synagogue at Capernaum, before he was yet known as a preacher or worker of miracles, a man with an unclean spirit cried out, saying, "What have we to do with thee, thou Jesus of Nazareth? art thou come to destroy us? I know thee who thou art, the Holy One of God".[6] Similarly of the Gerasene demoniac it is said that "when he saw Jesus from afar, he ran and worshipped

---

[1] Mark viii. 33; *cf.* Matt. iv. 10. [2] Luke xxii. 3.
[3] Luke xxii. 31. [4] Mark iii. 23, 26.
[5] iii. 27. [6] i. 24.

him; and crying out with a loud voice, he saith, "What have I to do with thee, Jesus, thou Son of the Most High God? I adjure thee by God, torment me not"; and there follows an extraordinary conversation between Jesus and the spirits, in which he shows understanding without sympathy, and enmity without animosity—as though both sides had taken it for granted that the good spirit must destroy the bad, but wished to arrange the matter with as little unpleasantness as possible.[1] These are not isolated instances, for in two summaries of Jesus' miracles (few of which were ever recorded in detail) a special note is made as to his dealing with spirits. Thus "he healed many that were sick with divers diseases, and cast out many devils; and he suffered not the devils to speak, because they knew him":[2] and again, "the unclean spirits, whensoever they beheld him, fell down before him, and cried, saying, thou art the Son of God. And he charged them that they should not make him known."[3]

(iii) Whatever the extent of his "understanding with the powers of evil," Jesus never doubts that he can and must "cast out devils" whenever he has an opportunity; and he is sure that

[1] Mark v. 6-12.   [2] i. 34.   [3] iii. 11, 12.

JESUS' MIND

his power to do this is good and divine. The early miracles of Jesus—and particularly, it is implied, the cure of those "possessed"—having caused much discussion, the scribes try to attribute them to the powers of evil themselves working through Jesus: "he hath Beelzebub, and by the prince of the devils casteth he out the devils". Jesus' answer is negatively that Satan cannot cast out Satan, and positively (though this is rather implied than stated) that his own power comes from the Holy Spirit.[1] At the same time, he does not seem to claim for himself a different kind of power to that exercised by some other people, but only a higher degree of the same power. "He appointed twelve [the apostles] to have authority to cast out devils:"[2] "he gave them authority over unclean spirits";[3] and it is recorded that "they cast out many devils".[4] The failure of the disciples to work a cure in a particularly hard case implies that they generally succeeded.[5] And one case is reported in which the disciples found one who was not a follower of Jesus casting out devils in his name. Jesus, questioned about this, acknowledges that some men can "do a mighty work

[1] Mark iii. 22-30.   [2] iii. 15.   [3] vi. 7.
[4] vi. 13.   [5] ix. 18, 28.

in my name" without being disciples, and enjoins a charitable attitude towards them.[1]   In any arguments that are based on Jesus' miracles, this is a point that cannot be overlooked. He did not himself regard his miracles as unique or his powers as incommunicable.

One may now sum up certain conclusions as to Jesus' demonology.

(i) The spirits are of various kinds—"unclean," "dumb," and the like; though these particular symptoms do not exhaust the malignity of the "possession". To have a "dumb spirit" is more than to be dumb.

(ii) The spirits are apparently silent and powerless except when inhabiting a body. Jesus has no dealings with spirits invisible to others, but only with recognised cases of "possession". Spirits can be sent away "out of the country" into some kind of exile;[2] or they can be transferred into the bodies of animals, but with results disastrous to the animals.[3]

(iii) They do violence to the bodies which they inhabit in various ways. The demoniac of Gerasa "had his dwelling in the tombs," and resisted all attempts to confine him; "and always,

[1] Mark ix. 38-40.   [2] Mark v. 10.   [3] v. 12, 13.

night and day, in the tombs and in the mountains, he was crying out, and cutting himself with stones".[1] Of the "dumb spirit" that possessed a boy it is said that "Wheresoever it taketh him, it dasheth him down; and he foameth, and grindeth his teeth, and pineth away".[2]

(iv) They recognise Jesus, claiming (it seems) kinship as spirits, but knowing that he is good, they evil. His presence gives them speech, and makes them reasonable, so that they answer questions, make requests, or obey commands.[3] Sometimes it has the opposite effect, leading to fresh outbreaks of violence.[4] In either case it brings their activity to a head.

(v) With greater or less difficulty Jesus can always "cast them out". He can do it either absolutely, or by transference into another body; he can do it by his simple word, either close by or at a distance;[5] in special cases there is also a need of prayer.[6]

(vi) Lastly, a considerable degree of this power over evil spirits can be delegated by Jesus to his disciples; and similar miracles can be worked in his name by some who are not even his followers.

These points probably represent Jesus'

[1] Mark v. 3-5. [2] ix. 18. [3] v. 6-12. [4] ix. 20.
[5] v. 11, 12; cf. Matt. viii. 30. [6] ix. 29.

main ideas about the powers of evil. They are not theoretical, but experimental: they constitute a diagnosis which may not have been scientific, but which corresponded roughly to the facts, and justified itself in practice. Jesus was not peculiar in his experience. It was shared by many others who practised gifts of healing, and by multitudes who benefited by them; it has been shared to some extent by spiritually-minded or superstitious men of every age; and it is claimed by the "spiritual healers" of the present day[1]. To many of these people "obsession" is a real phenomenon, and the power of disease and evil in the worst cases is something personal, though alien and hostile to the person affected. Jesus, perhaps, felt this alien power more intensely than others, and dealt with it more confidently and completely: but in that alone lies, in this respect, his uniqueness.

VI

There is a general agreement between the Synoptic evangelists that a considerable part of Jesus' teaching was eschatological. All three

---

[1] To be spiritually-minded when one might be scientific is the essence of superstition. The modern spiritual healers cannot claim the example of Jesus. He was as scientific as he could be: they are not.

JESUS' MIND

gospels give, among the incidents of the last week of the ministry, an eschatological discourse. It is introduced in the same way; and it consists, in spite of some dislocations and additions, of essentially the same matter. It is not certain—indeed, it is unlikely—that Jesus really spoke all these things on one occasion: more probably they represent a very early compilation, which was perhaps in circulation before even the second gospel was written: but at any rate it is safe to assume that Jesus did throw much of his teaching into this form. In this he followed a common trend of Jewish thought: his originality consisted in his vivid apprehension and personal appropriation of the rather intangible images of the Jewish apocalypses.

The apparent confusedness of the discourse in the second gospel is due to the fact that it deals with three subjects which, in Jesus' thought perhaps, and certainly in the minds of those who have reported him, were not kept distinct—namely, the Fall of Jerusalem, the early Christian persecutions, and the Second Coming of the Messiah. Yet this confusedness may easily be exaggerated. In its original form, which is less concealed in S. Mark's version than in the others, the discourse seems to have consisted of three sections, each dealing with one of the three main subjects. But this arrangement has been spoilt by the unskilful addition of detached sayings, whose exact reference had been lost, or never discovered: hence the present disorder of the passage.[1]

This confusedness is to some extent natural in such a discourse. There is very little sense of time or space about it. It is almost a dream. These things were very real to Jesus: but the forms under which they came to him were quite inadequate to express them; and there is a sense of distant perspectives behind the solid foreground of the vision which makes it very difficult to keep the whole in focus. Moreover, although Jesus himself may have kept the three events distinct from one another, he certainly regarded them as close to one another in point of time; and it is not even certain in what order he anticipated their happening. This of course increases the confusion.

The chief point that emerges from this rather difficult body of evidence is that Jesus imagined the things which he predicted to be very near at hand. It is true, he said in one connection (the passage as a whole seems to refer to the Christian persecutions), "The Gospel must first

[1] Mark xiii.; *cf.* Matt. xxiv., Luke xxi.

be preached unto all nations":[1] but what was Jesus' idea of "all nations"? how far would it be covered by the Jews of the Dispersion who were present at Pentecost? or if it was a wider conception, how long a time was contemplated? The saying is at any rate balanced, and probably quite outweighed, by those others which are introduced by the emphatic, "Verily I say unto you"—"This generation shall not pass away, until all these things be accomplished,"[2] and "Verily I say unto you, there be some here of them that stand by, which shall in no wise taste of death, till they see the kingdom of God come with power".[3] That is to say, the *terminus ad quem* of the events that Jesus foresaw he placed within the lifetime of his hearers. All three events, the Fall of Jerusalem, the Christian Persecution, and the displacement of the present order of things by the coming of the Messiah and the establishment of the kingdom of God, were to happen within, or almost within, the first century A.D. Jerusalem, as a matter of fact, fell in the year 70. Persecutions preceded and followed it. The Church waited, patiently and hopefully, year after year, for the fulfilment of the third part of the prophecy. But it never came. "Of that

---

[1] Mark xiii. 10.   [2] xiii. 30.   [3] ix. 1.

day or that hour," Jesus had certainly said, "knoweth no one, not even the angels in heaven, neither the Son, but the Father:"[1] but this apparently meant no more than ignorance of the exact time of an event which was expected to fall within certain limits, namely, the life-time of the first generation of Christians. That was how the disciples interpreted it. Were they wrong? Or was their error, with all its effects, both passing and permanent, upon the form and spirit of the Church, due to some misunderstanding on the part of Jesus himself? Or are we thrown back again upon the hypothesis that Jesus used the popular Messianic language, with its expectation of a speedy deliverance, because he could use no other, and knowing it to be quite inadequate?

If one asks a little more in detail what were Jesus' opinions as to the life beyond death, one finds some such indications as the following:—

(i) Jesus did not share the ordinary opinion that death is the end of life. Death, he thought, is sleep.[2] For himself it is the condition of

---

[1] Mark xiii. 32.

[2] v. 39 (unless it be taken literally, and we suppose that the child was really in a trance).

winning the new life of the kingdom. For his disciples the way to find life is to lose it. Hardly any idea is more essential to Jesus' thought than this. Yet nothing is said as to what kind of change or transition takes place during the sleep of death.

(ii) Jesus seems to have shared popular notions on the subject of reincarnation. As Herod's theory about Jesus was that "John, whom I beheaded, is risen from the dead,"[1] and as it was popularly supposed that he was the Baptist, or Elijah, or one of the prophets come to life again,[2] so Jesus himself was sure that the Baptist was a reincarnation of Elijah: "I say unto you, that Elijah is come, and they have also done unto him whatsoever they listed".[3]

(iii) The nature of the future life is expressed in curiously materialistic language, the inadequacy of which was perhaps more evident to Jesus himself than to his hearers: "To sit on my right hand or on my left hand is not mine to give: but it is for them for whom it hath been prepared";[4] or again: "The Son of man ... cometh in the glory of his Father with the holy angels";[5] "and then shall they see the Son

[1] Mark vi. 14, 16.   [2] viii. 28.   [3] ix. 13.
[4] x. 40.   [5] viii. 38.

of man coming in clouds with great power and glory. And then shall he send forth the angels, and shall gather together his elect from the four winds, from the uttermost part of the earth to the uttermost part of heaven;"[1] and lastly: "I will no more drink of the fruit of the vine, until that day when I drink it new in the Kingdom of God".[2]

(iv) In one passage at least we have the other side of the picture. "It is good for thee," says Jesus, "to enter into life maimed, rather than having thy two hands to go into hell, into the unquenchable fire. . . . It is good for thee to enter into life halt, rather than having thy two feet to be cast into hell. . . . It is good for thee to enter into the Kingdom of God with one eye, rather than having two eyes to be cast into hell; where their worm dieth not, and the fire is not quenched."[3] The language is again figurative and materialistic, and in part borrowed from Isaiah. But there can be no doubt as to the reality, in Jesus' mind, of the state which is contrasted with "life". The words that immediately follow—"For every one shall be salted with fire" —may introduce a further purgatorial idea into

---

[1] Mark xiii. 26, 27. [2] xiv. 25. [3] ix. 43-47.

JESUS' MIND

the passage : but perhaps they are a detached saying, put here as dealing with " fire," just as the sayings which follow are grouped together because they deal with " salt ".[1]

We come then to the same kind of conclusion with regard to Jesus' eschatology as we reached in dealing with his demonology and his treatment of Scripture. The main content and form of his eschatology were shared by his contemporaries : his uniqueness lay in the clearness with which he saw what to others was vague and misty, and the personal application which he found in the common stock of apocalypses. To Jesus the present world was less substantial than the future : all life here must be sacrificed, if need be, for a footing there. And the great hypothesis of his life, which only death could verify, was always in his mind— that in him all the prophecies of Scripture found their fulfilment, as the long-expected Messiah.

VII

We have already dealt in some detail with the methods of Jesus' teaching. Our present inquiry only concerns such evidence as may be

[1] Mark ix. 49, 50.

drawn from those methods as to Jesus' habitual ways of thought.

(i) One of the most obvious of these is the dependence of Jesus' ideas upon concrete facts. He believed supremely in the argument of acts. Acts suggested thoughts to him, as pen and paper do to many people. His mind was in close contact with the common experiences of every-day life, and built its teaching upon knowledge of men, and men's affairs. It was always ready to pass from concrete particulars to spiritual principles. An obvious instance is the incident of the widow's mites:[1] many others have been or could be quoted.[2]

(ii) Jesus thought, as he spoke, in aphorisms. He liked to conceive big definite principles. His mind could hold both sides of a question, but was happier in developing either side to its full value than in balancing one against the other. Its power lay in the quality of its thinking, the enthusiasm of its belief, along certain rather definite lines. After a certain point, to be wide-minded is to be weak-minded. And so Jesus' thoughts expressed themselves in sayings that are not mere epigrams but have permanently enriched and inspired the world.[3]

[1] Mark xii. 41-44. [2] *Cf.* p. 44. [3] *Cf.* p. 46.

(iii) Jesus did not as a rule argue with people, or try to produce convictions of reason. He more often made dogmatic statements, and relied upon his personal authority to prove them. The only form of argument generally recognised which he used at all habitually was the argument from analogy. This underlies more or less consciously both his metaphorical sayings and his parables. Indeed metaphor and analogy are so habitual with him that one may reasonably suspect their presence in sayings which in form, at any rate, allow a literal interpretation. Towards the end of his ministry, when he was convicting rather than converting his hearers, Jesus may have used directer arguments:[1] when he wished to convert them he used the argument for analogy.

(iv) Jesus very seldom criticised other men, or their opinions. The only great exception to this rule was in the case of the official religious parties—the scribes, whose interpretation of a psalm he questioned;[2] the Sadducees, who were in great error as regards the future life;[3] and the Pharisees, whose "tradition" was a transgression of the commandment of God.[4] Even in such cases

---

[1] Mark xii. 26, 27, 35-37.   [2] xii. 35-37.
[3] xii. 26, 27.   [4] vii. 6-13.

the criticism of a wrong view generally leads to a statement of the right one; just as, again, questions put by disciples or others are not merely answered, but are turned into the teaching of positive principles.[1] Jesus came not to criticise, but to create.

(v) Again, he did not care for definitions, or detailed applications of thought: and he was thus able to keep clear of the complications which come from a premature confusion of principle and practice, particular and universal. His avoidance of moral casuistry might be illustrated by his treatment of the rich young ruler,[2] his independence of political parties by his answer about the tribute to Cæsar,[3] and his abstraction from religious controversy by his conversation with the Sadducees.[4]

(vi) Finally, Jesus' method of teaching is marked on one or two occasions by that splendid unreason of which only the strongest minds are capable. His question to the synagogue folk, who "watched him, whether he would heal ... on the Sabbath day," is a case in point. "Is it lawful," he said, "on the Sabbath day to do good, or to do harm? to save a life, or to kill?" This

[1] Mark x. 35-45; xii. 13-17, 18-27.   [2] Mark x. 17-22.
[3] xii. 13-17.   [4] xii. 18-27.

JESUS' MIND

was, strictly speaking, *nil ad rem:* the question was, Why do *anything*? But it went to the root of the matter: there could be no answer to it: "they held their peace".[1] Or, again, when the question was put, "Is it lawful to give tribute unto Cæsar, or not?" Jesus' answer begged the whole question, by assuming that a coinage with Cæsar's head on it was Cæsar's property.[2] But, like some other logical fallacies, it was true and unanswerable.

VIII

Below the surface of the Gospel, beneath the crude and inadequate forms in which Jesus embodied his thoughts and teaching, one feels more and more the working of a wonderfully true and powerful mind—a mind true by superior insight, rather than by the balancing of "*pros*" and "*cons*"; a mind powerful, sometimes, by its very outrage of reason; a mind that convinces by its certainty and authoritativeness. Is not this what the Incarnation, so far as Jesus' mind is concerned, must have meant—not the addition to a natural consciousness of some supernatural qualities, nor any incongruous mixture of human and divine, where each element is re-

[1] Mark iii. 1-4. [2] xii. 13-17.

garded as independent and "ready-made," but the successful emergence of the human mind from within its own limitations, and the achievement of the mastery that proves it divine? The essence of divinity, as of all life, lies not so much in special forms of manifestation as in a power of growth.

We ought not to hesitate to use the word "growth" of Jesus' mind, if we can use it of his body. It is a fallacy to suppose that the higher faculties of man are discredited by the lowliness of their origin, or the gradualness of their growth. We are making the same mistake if we expect the divine quality of Jesus' mind to be shown in sudden superhuman achievements, or if we deny that it can have emerged gradually from and through lower stages of intellectual growth.

CHAPTER V

JESUS' SOCIAL OUTLOOK

I

IN our badly organised society, which is gradually becoming conscious of its disorder, few questions are more debated than the relation of Christianity to social problems. This large issue we are not called upon to discuss; but it ought to be possible, upon our present line of argument, to throw some light on the smaller question, What was the attitude of Jesus towards social problems? To answer the latter question is not necessarily, as we shall see, to answer the former; but at least the inquiry must be of the highest interest and importance.

It will be necessary to ask, first of all, how far Jesus was limited by nationality and class in respect to these questions; what, if any, were his social presuppositions or prejudices. Secondly, we shall wish to know what line he took as to such big questions as Wealth, or the Family, or the State. Thirdly, we should inquire what, if any, would be his methods of social reform. And fourthly, we must try to get a clear idea as to what he meant by the Kingdom of God.

II

The influences of family and home must have been exceedingly strong in Jesus' case. For thirty years, which included the most impressionable periods of childhood and youth, he lived an uneventful home life in a hill-town of Galilee. Difficult as it may be to reconstruct the influences of the home life at Nazareth, one cannot doubt, working on some such lines as we have laid down,[1] that they must have had an intense effect upon Jesus' character and ideas. The fact that his own people rejected him, and he them, when the claims of religion cut across the traditions of home, shows that there was nothing which Jesus was not ready to sacrifice to religious enthusiasm: but he could not on that account escape, nor would he wish to escape, from the subtle but powerful influences of his past life upon his present.

One of those influences continued to act upon

[1] *Cf.* p. 20.

him throughout his ministry through the persons of his habitual friends. The poorer a man is, the quieter his home, and the smaller his circumstances, the less is it possible for him to pick his own friends. Birth and neighbourhood choose them for him. In Jesus' case there was, no doubt, a definite call of certain men to become disciples: but we have seen reasons for thinking that some of these, at any rate, were already relatives or friends: and in any case Jesus' habitual companions are sufficiently of one class to make one look behind the time of the ministry for the reasons for their selection.

The class most largely represented among the inner circle of followers was that of fishermen on the lake of Galilee. Peter and Andrew, James and John, certainly belonged to this profession, with which, next to his own, Jesus is likely to have had most contact during his early life. Bartholomew and Levi were also Galileans, perhaps old friends; the latter was one of the unpopular class of tax-collectors. Five if not six of the twelve have nick-names, and may have been on terms of special familiarity with Jesus—James and John the "Sons of Thunder," Simon "the Rock," Thomas "the Twin," Simon "the Zealot," and perhaps James "the Small".

Of only one of the number can we say that he was probably not a Galilean—Judas of Kerioth beyond Jordan.[1] For none can we with any certainty claim wealth, or position, or good birth. They must have been chosen partly for their piety; but principally, perhaps, because they were men of Jesus' own social class, whom he could trust and lead and inspire. Jesus "loved" the rich young ruler,[2] and told the scribe that he was "not far from the Kingdom of God";[3] but as disciples they would not have suited his purpose, any more than the poor Gerasene whom he sent home to his house and to his friends.[4]

It must have been due in some degree to his upbringing that Jesus became known as "a friend of publicans and sinners,"[5] a title justified by at least one incident in the second gospel. A publican was one of his earliest disciples, and at Levi's house great scandal was caused among the pious because "many publicans and sinners sat down with Jesus and his disciples: for there were many, and they followed him". Jesus' answer is at least in part ironical—"I came not to call the righteous [as the pious ob-

---

[1] Mark iii. 16-19.   [2] x. 21.   [3] xii. 34.
[4] v. 18-19.   [5] Luke vii. 34.

jectors think themselves] but sinners"; yet it also represents the practical policy which was laid down for his Ministry by social presuppositions as well as religious needs. Jesus moved most naturally among the poor, of whom he was one himself.[1]

III

If one turns from Jesus' friends to his enemies, one finds that the opposition into which he was habitually forced against the "scribes and Pharisees," was at least in part due to social influences.

(i) In the first place, he shared to the full the Galilean "provincial" feeling against the more extreme claims of the Judæan priesthood; and that, together with the native nonconformity of his intensely spiritual religion, made it almost inevitable that he should be regarded as the leader of a reform movement hostile to the hierarchy of Jerusalem. Thus the visit to Jerusalem with which the ministry ends loses much of its point in the second gospel unless it is the first visit of a provincial prophet to the centre of his religion. Jesus is described as spending his first day sight-seeing in the Temple, as a stranger

[1] Mark ii. 14-17.

might :[1] the cleansing of the Temple the next day is done in indignation at a state of things not hitherto realised :[2] the Jerusalem crowd is "astonished at his teaching," as the Galileans had been when he first appeared at Capernaum :[3] at the betrayal, Judas has to give his followers a sign by which they may know Jesus :[4] and at the trial the isolation of Jesus, and the credibility of the accusation made by the false witnesses, rests on the fact that Jesus and his disciples are a small body of provincial enthusiasts among a mass of hostile official opinion—[5] a view which is borne out by the dispersion which follows Jesus' arrest,[6] the fear which drove S. Peter to denial,[7] the flight to Galilee,[8] and the secrecy surrounding the evidences of the Resurrection.

(ii.) At the same time Jesus represented more than a provincial view. Himself a member of the "pious poor" class, he stood for a growing feeling on the part of the really religious against the pretensions of the officially religious party, and his hostility to the authorities at Jerusalem was largely the expression of popular feeling both within and without the city. When Jesus

[1] This seems to be the meaning of xi. 11.

[2] Mark xi. 15. But this account is perhaps not inconsistent with Jesus' having visited Jerusalem in the days *before* his ministry. [3] xi. 18; *cf.* i. 27. [4] xiv. 44. [5] xiv.

[6] xiv. 50-52. [7] xiv. 66-72. [8] xvi. 7.

JESUS' SOCIAL OUTLOOK

openly attacks the administration of the Temple, taking the law into his own hands, no steps are taken against him, because popular feeling is on his side.[1] When he turns back upon the priests their challenge of his authority, "they feared the people," who took the Baptist, and therefore Jesus also, for a prophet.[2] They made no answer to a parable obviously directed against themselves; for "they feared the multitude".[3] And it is recorded that, when Jesus controverted the scribes' interpretation of a Messianic psalm, "the common people heard him gladly," so that he pressed home the attack with an open denunciation of the scribes.[4]

No doubt it was primarily on religious grounds that Jesus found himself out of sympathy with the official representatives of religion : but it also appears that something which might come under the head of social presuppositions played no small part in his attitude.

One may add some slight indications that Jesus shared the Jewish attitude of exclusiveness towards the Gentiles. It may be nothing that Gentile methods of government are held up as an example to be avoided by the disciples in their

[1] Mark xi. 15-18. [2] xi. 27-33.
[3] xii. 12. [4] xii. 35-40.

own relationship:[1] but there is certainly some significance in Jesus' treatment of the heathen woman of Syro-Phœnicia. "The children," that is, the Jews, are first to be filled: "the dogs," that is, the Gentiles, may have what crumbs fall from the children's table. This was quite consistent with the reasons which had brought Jesus into those parts. He wished to be free for a time from the responsibility and fatigue of his ministry. He had no message for the heathen.[2]

IV

So much for presuppositions. It seems best, in the next place, to try to estimate the attitude which Jesus took up with regard to the great social relationships which depend upon wealth, and family life, and the State. It should be possible in each of these cases to trace some part of the principles or theories underlying Jesus' social dealings.

(i) One of the best-known incidents in the gospel bears directly upon the problem of wealth. A man described by S. Mark as "one that had great possessions," by S. Matthew as "a young man," and by S. Luke as "a certain ruler," came to Jesus, with every mark of reverence, and asked

[1] Mark x. 42. [2] vii. 24-30.

him what he should do to "inherit eternal life" —that is, to become a subject of the Kingdom of God. It is clear that the man was a good man, a conscientious observer of the whole law of righteousness. But this does not qualify him for the Kingdom. "One thing thou lackest," is Jesus' answer; "Go, sell whatsoever thou hast, and give to the poor, and thou shalt have treasure in heaven : and come, follow me."[1]

Jesus' main object is to show that true religion demands more than can be given by the best morality—*viz.*, an enthusiasm of self-sacrifice. In this particular case the self that needed to be sacrificed was the man's *habit of being rich*. (One need not suppose, from the man's unreadiness to take Jesus' advice, that he was over-fond of his wealth : many rich people, who are not that, would nevertheless be quite unable to do without their money.) Wealth, as indeed appears from the sequel,[2] includes home, relations, and lands, that is, all the ordinary sentiments and indulgences of society. To sacrifice wealth is to sacrifice social intercourse with the world. Jesus, however, claimed this absolute surrender. He had made it himself, and had taught the necessity of it to his disciples. So it was not merely be-

[1] Mark x. 17-22.   [2] x. 29.

cause of this man's special circumstances that he claimed it now, but because he regarded voluntary poverty as a general condition of spiritual growth—as a normal requirement of membership of the Kingdom of God.

It appears, further, that Jesus did not share the ordinary views as to the nature of wealth. Wealth, we should say, is a power of exchange, which may be used either well or ill, and which, according to its use, can enormously help or hinder spiritual development. Rightly applied, wealth gives some of the finest faculties and opportunities for influence, beauty, knowledge; and, in contrast to it, poverty becomes almost a crime. But there is nothing of this idea in Jesus' treatment of the question. He regards wealth as something inherently deceitful and obstructive; something which so nearly excludes its possessors from eternal life that a material miracle were easier than the moral one of their admission to it.[1] True wealth, on the other hand, is purely spiritual, and is to be won only by the complete renunciation of worldly riches.[2]

(ii) A second incident which bears on the same subject is the question about the Imperial Tribute.[3] Here again Jesus shows the same

[1] Mark x. 23-25. [2] x. 29-30. [3] xii. 13-17.

misunderstanding of the nature of money on which we remarked above. To him a coin is not a medium of exchange, but something the value of which lies in itself, and which is the property of the person whose "image and superscription" are stamped upon it. And, again, there is the same clear distinction between the things of God and the things of Cæsar, between spiritual and worldly wealth, which underlay his treatment of the rich young man. (For it is more natural to take this as Jesus' normal point of view than as a temporary concession to the ideas of his audience.)

(iii) The same principles reappear in the incident of the widow's mites. Jesus shows his instinctive distrust of riches by his attitude towards the offerings of the rich folk, and his approval of voluntary poverty by his blessing on the poor widow's deliberate self-beggary. There is again the feeling that money is somehow in itself bad, and that it is best to be rid of it as soon as may be.[1]

(iv) Even more significant is Jesus' treatment of the incident of his anointing at Bethany.[2] A woman buys an expensive flask of the

---

[1] Mark xii. 41-44. [2] xiv. 3-9.

finest ointment, and "wastes" it by pouring it on Jesus' head, as a sign of reverence and a symbol of his kingship. "She hath done what she could," says Jesus; so perhaps here too it was "all her living".

One expects Jesus to protest. His disciples do so, repeating the advice that he had given to the rich young man—"This should have been sold, and given to the poor". But Jesus sees something behind the object of the gift, namely the spirit of the giver: that is the supremely important thing; if that is right, the act is perfect. The surrender of wealth is good, in any case: but this is something more; and the act is immortalised. Incidentally, it is noticeable that Jesus definitely rejects the disciples' suggestion of the "exchange value" of the ointment.

"Ye have the poor always with you, and whensoever ye will ye can do them good"— these words, in which Jesus defends the woman's choice of the object of her charity, are descriptive, not legislative. They do not sanction a state of society which involves poverty; neither do they prescribe philanthropy. They simply state Jesus' conception of the world as a society of fixed classes—the rich and the poor, or those who give charity and those who receive it.

This conception was a part of his heritage, a result of his experience. He accepted society as he found it, and did not seriously think of it as likely to be changed.

We should say, then, of Jesus' view as a whole, that it is a very forcible statement of one side of the case; and that, though the exceptional enthusiast may become rich in spiritual things in proportion as he becomes poor in worldly possessions, yet the ordinary man will only be weaker, narrower, and worse for the surrender of the faculties of living. The demand for voluntary poverty is, in fact, a fanatical demand, which the Church has not seen fit to repeat except in special cases.

It seems, indeed, that we can neither claim the authority of Jesus for the ordinary teaching of the Church on this subject, nor the sanction of the Church for the ordinary teaching of Jesus. Yet this is one of several cases in which it is most desirable that a clearer idea should be arrived at as to what Christianity really demands. Was Jesus right, or is the Church right? Is the Kingdom of God to be won by the proper use of wealth, or by the surrender of it? If by the latter, we must reconsider our whole attitude as Christians towards the institution of property;

if by the former, let us at any rate not quote Jesus' words or example to support an attitude which was not his own.

V

Two facts have to be borne in mind, which probably go some way towards accounting for Jesus' views on the subject of family life. First, after thirty years of home life, he deliberately renounced it all for the sake of religion. And secondly, he was himself unmarried.

(i) The marriage law was twice a subject of discussion between Jesus and his opponents. On one occasion the Pharisees "tempted" him with a question about divorce: what view did he take about the Mosaic law, which, under certain circumstances, permitted a husband to divorce his wife? Jesus, who (as a Jew) takes monogamy for granted, regards the Mosaic law as a concession made because of men's "hardness of heart," and would go back to the ideal of indissoluble marriage which lies behind it. He does not announce this as a new law, but restores it as the proper interpretation of the old. But he stands quite clearly for a higher ideal of family life than most of his contemporaries thought necessary. "What God hath joined together, let not man put asunder."[1]

It follows, as a corollary from this, that the meaning of the law against adultery must be very much enlarged. Its prohibition extends not merely to technical breaches of the Mosaic compromise, but also to all offences against the higher ideal. The second gospel knows nothing of the saving clause which has been inserted by S. Matthew. "Whosoever," it simply says, "shall put away his wife, and marry another, committeth adultery against her: and if she herself shall put away her husband, and marry another, she committeth adultery."[2]

In making this interpretation of the Jewish law of marriage and divorce Jesus was not consciously legislating for any society. It is unfair to treat his words as though he were so doing. Further, in falling back on this ideal, he is also falling back on the authority of the Book of Genesis, which, in common with his contemporaries, he regarded as final. But an ideal is an ideal, whatever its origin and form of expression. And Jesus' ideal of family life is able to override any laws which society may make to facilitate divorce, as easily as it can, in case

[1] Mark x. 2-9.   [2] x. 11-12; *cf.* Matt. v. 32, xix. 9.

of need, ignore the traditional sanctions and respectabilities by which society professes to sustain the institution of marriage.

(ii) Another side of Jesus' attitude towards marriage is shown by his discussion with the Sadducees, arising out of a question which was intended to throw discredit upon the reality of the life after death. Here Jesus accepts without criticism the rather peculiar provisions of the Levirate law of marriage (with its frank avowal that marriage is primarily for the sake of procreation): but he can do so just because he regards all marriage as a temporary expedient, a purely worldly affair, that has no reality outside the conditions of the present life: " When they shall rise from the dead, they neither marry, nor are given in marriage; but are as angels in heaven ".[1] He does not deal at all with the difficulty of the transition from this life to that, or with the problems that can be raised as to the continuance of personal relationships and recognitions in a future life. To him the present existence does not merge into the future, but is deeply sundered from it—in his own case, by the Passion and death which are now so imminent; for the Jewish nation, by the fall of Jerusalem;

[1] Mark xii. 18-25.

JESUS' SOCIAL OUTLOOK

for his disciples, by the cup and baptism of persecution that they will have to share; for mankind as a whole, by the coming catastrophe of the end of the world.

(iii) Although the only passage in the gospel that deals directly with a man's duty towards his family is that which approves the complete renunciation of family ties for the sake of religion,[1] yet there are many signs of Jesus' particular care and reverence for children. Three children are specially mentioned as being healed by him:[2] in doing kindness to a child, he says, one is doing kindness to himself:[3] better any offence than that against "one of these little ones":[4] the faith and simplicity of children is a pattern of the character of true discipleship:[5] twice Jesus is described as taking children into his arms,[6] and once as laying his hand upon them and blessing them.[7] Childless men are often the most fond of children; and children trust a good man. But Jesus' way with children is a sign, too, of his high ideal of family life.

On the whole, the most remarkable thing in

---

[1] Mark x. 29.   [2] v. 42; vii. 25; ix. 24.   [3] ix. 37.
[4] ix. 42 (but "little ones" here might mean "disciples").
[5] x. 15.   [6] ix. 36; x. 16.   [7] x. 16.

Jesus' attitude towards family life is his silence upon so many questions which have seemed of special importance to Christians. There is no discussion, so far as the second gospel is concerned, of the expediency or otherwise of marriage; nothing about the duties of family relationship; nothing about the training of children. For those who remain in the world there is the ideal of indissoluble marriage: for those who would be disciples there is the higher ideal of complete renunciation: in the real world—the life of the kingdom of God—" they neither marry nor are given in marriage; but are as angels in heaven".

VI

Only once in the second gospel does Jesus deal with a political question. Either as a sign of the co-operation of hostile parties against Jesus, or in order to give colour to their request for a decision, representatives of the pro-Roman and anti-Roman parties wait upon him, and ask his opinion on the political question of the day—" Is it lawful to give tribute unto Cæsar, or not? shall we give, or shall we not give?"[1]

[1] Mark xii. 13-15.

The question is prefaced with a remarkable tribute to Jesus' independence of politics. "Master," they say, "we know that thou art true [that is, unbiassed], and carest not for any one: for thou regardest not the person of men [that is, he is known as one who is independent of parties, and takes his own line], but of a truth teachest the way of God [religion, not politics, being his main "interest"].[1] This is significant evidence as to Jesus' ordinary attitude towards one of the most absorbing preoccupations of his countrymen.

Jesus answers the question with an aphorism at once so true and so irrelevant that it cannot possibly be answered. So far as this bears on his idea of wealth, it has already been discussed.[2] As regards politics, it suggests a dualistic conception of Church and State, in which "the things that are Cæsar's" are sharply distinguished from "the things that are God's"—unless, indeed, Jesus' meaning is that the lesser allegiance owed to the State is completely swallowed up in the larger duty to God.[3]

It would be unfair to draw very wide inferences from evidence as scanty and disputable as this is. The most certain point is that Jesus

[1] Mark xii. 14.   [2] *Cf.* p. 118.   [3] xii. 15-17.

took little or no interest in political questions. The issue of the Messiahship was to him a purely religious one. The kingdom of God was not to be brought about by any political readjustments. The new world was to be won, not by the reformation, but by the abolition of the old. To one who lived in such ideas political questions would be of little account.

Nor can one find any interest on Jesus' part in other "social questions". Partly, such problems did not exist then—not because there were no social ills, but because the idea of social as distinct from political change had hardly entered men's minds; partly, Jesus' preoccupation was so entirely with religion that he ignored the spiritual influence of social conditions in the same kind of way as he ignored the spiritual value of wealth.

VII

If, then, it appears that, as regards social matters, Jesus accepted the *status quo*, it becomes unprofitable to inquire what were his methods of social reform. Certainly one method of philanthropy, which the world is apt to regard as reformative, was never so treated by him. Charity was, in Jesus' view, the best way of spending money—but never as a method of reform, always as a step in the path towards holiness. In this, Jesus was perhaps wiser than the present generation: for it is not the giving of money, but the idea that one can do good by giving it, that does so much harm. At the same time, regarding charity frankly as a part of religion, Jesus did not encumber it with conditions which might spoil its spontaneity, without very much increasing its efficiency. His own charity of good deeds and words was given ungrudgingly to all who asked or needed it—often (it must have been) without "inquiry" or guarantee of good use—for simple love of God and man.[1] In the same lavish way he gives entertainment to crowds four or five thousand strong, providing (it is reported) by supernatural means the food which he would as willingly have purchased, if it had been possible, out of the common fund.[2] To the rich young ruler he gives the advice, "sell whatsoever thou hast, and give to the poor"[3]— advice which the disciples had learnt to echo when they said, "This ointment might have been sold for above three hundred pence, and given to the poor".[4] Moreover the rule of poverty which

[1] *Cf.* p. 58. [2] vi. 35-38; viii. 1-5.
[3] x. 21. [4] xiv. 5.

Jesus prescribed to his apostles, necessitating as it did that they should beg for food and hospitality, not only encouraged charity in money and in kind : it also gave the highest sanction to the religious use of mendicancy, with all its attendant influences, bad as well as good.

Jesus' charity in fact was of the "old-fashioned" kind, which may be economically unsound, but which is in itself genuinely religious; which regards it as a duty to spend one's money in alms, and finds the normal way of doing so in indiscriminate gifts to the poor.

Excluding charity, and supposing that Jesus had been faced with the problem of social reform, can one at all say what methods he would have adopted? Only very tentatively can one suggest certain principles.

The change needed in those who are to become members of the Kingdom of God is revolutionary : they are to become children again :[1] the new life in them is to spring quickly from a very small seed to a very large growth.[2] And yet the change will come silently, gradually, unobserved—[3]evolutionary in method, revolutionary in result.

[1] Mark x. 15. [2] iv. 31, 32. [3] iv. 26-29.

Again, the influences that affect character, whether for good or for bad, are from within;[1] and this would seem to go against external reform. But, on the other hand, external causes of offence must be rigorously destroyed,[2] and it is useless to create a new spirit and then to expect it to be content with the old forms.[3]

And, lastly, great things can be done only by those who are first humble and then self-sacrificing. This, surely, the personal element, remains Jesus' unique contribution to social reform. Without it, no machinery or method can effect reform : with it, everything becomes possible.

VIII

There remains one conception which was quite central to Jesus' thoughts, and which must seriously affect our answer to the question under discussion. What did Jesus mean by the Kingdom of God? The phrase was constantly on his lips, the idea perpetually in his mind. Did he conceive it as something primarily religious? or social? or ecclesiastical? Was it to be a society, or a State, or a Church? Was it close at hand, or in the far future? in this world, or in a

[1] Mark vii. 20-23.   [2] ix. 43-48.   [3] ii. 21, 22.

world yet to come? Very various answers have been given to these questions: but since they have often been dictated as much by the dispositions of their authors as by the necessities of the evidence, and since in dealing with a single Gospel the amount of the evidence is not so overwhelming, it will be best not to accept any *a priori* decisions, but to try to form a new judgment from a short examination of all the passages in S. Mark which bear seriously upon the subject.

(1) i. 15. Jesus' first message to the world was "The time is fulfilled, and the Kingdom of God is at hand"—that is, the Messianic Kingdom, foretold by the prophets, and expected at the end of an appointed time.

(2) iv. 11. "Unto you is given the mystery of the Kingdom of God." Every Jew attached some meaning to the Kingdom of God. But the popular views regarded it as a national and political, as well as a religious ideal. Jesus did not publicly correct these false views, but in private he taught his disciples the true nature of the Messianic Kingdom—that it is a future and spiritual existence, a new life that can be won only by self-sacrifice, and suffering, and death.

(3) iv. 26-29. Jesus compares the Kingdom

of God to the grain which grows gradually, continuously, and inexplicably from seed-time to harvest. Or rather, the essential point of comparison is between the harvest and the coming of the Kingdom : the long period of growth in each case is preparatory for a definite future event.

(4) iv. 30-32. Another parable of growth, that of the mustard-seed, contrasts the humble beginning of the preaching of the Gospel with the greatness of the event to which it leads : or, more widely, it represents Jesus' faith that out of the present unpromising state of religion was to come nothing less than the Kingdom of God—though it was only in a spiritual sense that he could regard the former as passing on without a break into the latter.

(5) ix. 1. "There be some here of them that stand by, which shall in no wise taste of death, till they see the Kingdom of God come with power." This prediction is closely connected with the preceding description of the second coming of the Messiah, and clearly states that this event, and the establishment of the Messianic Kingdom, will take place within the life-time of some of the bystanders—*i.e.*, within, or almost within, the first century A.D.[1]

[1] *Cf.* p. 99.

(6) ix. 43-47. The Kingdom of God, called "life," is opposed to another state, called "hell," and is described as a future existence, to be won, if need be, at any sacrifice. Hand, foot, and eye, —the most precious faculties of life—are to be cut away if they imperil a man's entry into the Kingdom.

(7) x. 15. "Whosoever shall not receive the Kingdom of God as a little child, he shall in no wise enter therein." The Kingdom is not for every one, but demands a child-like faith and simplicity of those who would become subjects of it.

(8) x. 17-30. The rich young man who wishes to "inherit eternal life" means by that the Kingdom of God as Jesus preached it. To win "treasure in heaven," Jesus tells him, it is not enough to live blamelessly in this life: there must also be a complete surrender of worldly wealth. The Kingdom is something whose standards and values are quite different from those of this life. "How hardly shall they that have riches enter into the Kingdom of God! . . . It is easier for a camel to go through a needle's eye, than for a rich man to enter into the Kingdom of God." And it is clear that it is something quite outside the present life : those who become

JESUS' SOCIAL OUTLOOK

true disciples shall indeed receive present riches —of a spiritual kind; but the chief reward of their constancy is to be "in the world to come eternal life".

(9) x. 35-40. Two of the apostles (Jesus' cousins) ask to be allowed to sit on his right and left hand in his glory, that is, in his Kingdom. Jesus raises no objections to this rather materialistic view of the Kingdom, but reminds the disciples of the conditions of suffering and death through which alone the Kingdom can be won. As to the actual places in the Kingdom—the details of the future life—they are already settled, and not by himself but (he implies) by God. Here, again, is the same idea of the Kingdom as a definite future existence, though under unusually material forms: and it is interesting to get this indirect confirmation by the disciples of Jesus' direct teaching on the subject.

(10) xi. 10. "Blessed is the Kingdom that cometh, the Kingdom of our father David"—such was the acclamation of the crowd who accompanied Jesus at the time of his entry into Jerusalem. For the first time, Jesus seems to have allowed this public recognition. Few, probably, knew what kind of Messiahship he had come to claim, or through what strange experiences

the Kingdom was to be won. But for them all "the Kingdom"—once of David, now of the Christ—expressed, in the main, a common conception, a national ideal.

(11) xii. 34. To the scribe who answered him "discreetly" Jesus said, "Thou art not far from the Kingdom of God": some, who were not disciples, could be very like them in simplicity and faith.

(12) xiii. It is remarkable that the Kingdom of God is not actually mentioned in the eschatological discourse. But the coming of the Messiah, which is elsewhere so closely connected with the establishment of the Kingdom, must be held to be introductory to it here too. This coming is described in the figurative language of the Prophets: it is near at hand, though its exact time is not known: its circumstances and setting are of this world, but its significance is spiritual and other-worldly. The general sense of the discourse certainly requires a Kingdom that is "not of this world".

(13) xiv. 25. "I will drink no more of the fruit of the vine, until that day when I drink it new in the Kingdom of God." The literal meaning of this cannot be excluded, especially when one remembers the materialistic language used

of the Kingdom on other occasions. But "new" may mean "of a new kind," as well as "afresh"; and the saying may bear a secondary and more spiritual meaning. In any case the main contrast is between the present and the future states.

(14) xv. Throughout the trial of Jesus the most prominent point is his claim to be "the King of the Jews"; the title is constantly repeated: and he admits the claim. As a king he is mocked by the soldiers: it is his kingship which the chief priests deride: "Let Christ the King of Israel now come down from the cross". Nowhere is the irony of Jesus' position better shown: his kingship, in Pilate's sense and that of the priests, is a mockery and failure; but that is the appointed way to the real Kingship and the real Kingdom.

(15) xv. 43. Joseph of Arimathæa is described as one "who also himself was looking for the Kingdom of God". There were many such, not only among the upper classes (*cf.* (8) and (11) above), but also among the "pious poor". They shared Jesus' ideal, but perhaps disagreed with his personal claims, and his strange interpretation of the Messiahship.

Certain conclusions seem to follow from these passages.

(i) First, the Kingdom was not in any sense political and social, but simply and solely religious.

(ii) Secondly, although some of the above passages in isolation might reasonably be interpreted of membership in an already existent society, yet this was not Jesus' meaning. A moral preparation for the Kingdom was very necessary: but the Kingdom itself was an event lying wholly in the future.

(iii) It was in fact, the Messianic Kingdom, to which the old prophets looked forward, purged of its political limitations, and put quite outside the present order of things. This, and nothing else, is the meaning of the Kingdom of Heaven in the second gospel.

IX

Here, then, is our answer to the question, What was the relation of Jesus to social problems? And it is a rather startling one.

Jesus accepted the *status quo* of society, and used his healing powers, as he would have used money, indiscriminately, regarding charity as an exercise of religion, and not as a method of reform.

He took no interest in social questions as we

know them, and he thought that the present world was coming to an end in a few years.

His regenerated society, the Kingdom of God, was quite outside and alien to the present order of things, and entirely unworldly in its methods and constitution.

It follows that Jesus' principles, and the personal enthusiasm that he inspires, can be applied to social as well as to other problems, and may even be worked up into systems of Christian socialism, and the like: but that any such development will be outside the limits of Jesus' own authority and expectations.

Finally, whereas to the modern social reformer the present state of society is the only real and tangible one, and Utopias are the stuff of dreams, to Jesus the future life was the true reality, and the present world no more than the veil that must be rent before one can pass into the presence of God.

CHAPTER VI

JESUS' MORALITY

I

THE distinction that is sometimes made between religion and morality would have been quite meaningless to Jesus. It is clear that to him religion was everything, and that, though one may for the sake of convenience study his morality apart from it, yet the latter is, in fact, the spontaneous expression of the former in the sphere of conduct, and cannot really be separated from it.

It is often tacitly assumed that Jesus' morality means the Sermon on the Mount. Certainly that is the largest collection of ethical teachings in the gospels, and there is nothing comparable to it in S. Mark. But we shall expect to find all the essential principles of Jesus' morality in the scantier records of the second gospel, if it be in any sense a true biography. And, if these can be established, we shall be in a much stronger position for dealing with the more detailed teachings of the other gospels.

At the same time our object is not so much to explain Jesus' moral teaching as his morality—that is, his own moral principles and practice. This again, perhaps, is a distinction without a difference. But it suggests that much may be discovered from the less obvious sources of evidence: and it raises questions which are of immense importance with regard to Jesus' liability to temptation, and the meaning of his "sinlessness". But before coming to these subjects, something must be said as to the general nature of Jesus' morality, and its application to several important parts of life.

II

(i) In an important passage of his public teaching, arising out of a controversy with the Pharisees, Jesus lays down what appears to be the basis of all his moral principles.[1] "Hear me all of you, and understand: there is nothing from without the man, that going into him can defile him: but the things which proceed out of the man are those that defile the man." Immorality is not an act of defilement from without,

[1] Mark vii. 14-23.

but a motion of impurity from within; not an evil deed or circumstance that may cause an immoral thought, but an immoral thought that will, unless destroyed, give rise to all kinds of evil deeds and circumstances. Similarly, then, morality is a good thought, that works itself out in every kind of good deed.

If "evil thought" is the generic name for the vices which Jesus enumerated,[1] and "good thought" may be inferred as his class-name for the virtues, one naturally inquires whence these "thoughts" spring. The answer is, "from within, out of the heart of man";[2] and this seems to imply an identification of "the heart" with "the spirit,"—the spirit which is sometimes "willing" when the "flesh is weak".[3] It is a simple psychology, as one would expect. Its happiest definition lies in the words "from within" and "from without". But it expresses vividly enough the idea which was quite central in Jesus' morality—that the essence of goodness lies not in outward, but in inward conformity; not in the ritual of purification, but in the pure ablution of a good conscience.

(ii) Jesus experienced and taught the reality

---

[1] This seems to be the right interpretation of Mark vii. 21.
[2] Mark vii. 21.   [3] xiv. 38.

JESUS' MORALITY

of temptation. He knew the oppositeness of good and bad, and the choice involved in morality. And, whether or not he believed in a personal power of evil fighting against God,[1] at any rate, he had no doubt that it was often difficult to make a right choice in face of alternatives. His whole life was such a choice, in face of dire temptations. Tempted forty days in the desert;[2] tempted by his oldest friend as advocate of the fear of death,[3] tempted to shirk suffering, when he would not shirk death,[4] and tempted to doubt the very presence of God[5]—Jesus could realise very well the weakness that beset his friends,[6] and drove S. Peter to deny him.[7] The "best will in the world"—his own—could not remain untempted: his life was not a calm progress from perfection to perfection, but a real and constant struggle.

(iii) Natural feelings and emotions played a considerable part in Jesus' morality. He was easily moved to compassion, and so to acts of goodness—for instance, by the needs of a leper,[8] or by the sight of a great crowd that had come to

---

[1] *Cf.* p. 90.   [2] i. 13.   [3] viii. 33.
[4] xiv. 33-39: this is probably the meaning of the incident.
[5] xv. 34.   [6] xiv. 38.
[7] xiv. 30.   [8] i. 41.

hear him,[1] or by the hunger of the multitude.[2] Natural pity for a blind man,[3] and affection for children,[4] prompt small acts significant of much kindness. Peace[5] and forgiveness[6]—qualities most akin to natural love and good temper—are social virtues upon which he lays much stress.

(iv) Jesus never conceived morality merely as duty. It might involve temptation, and the stress of choice; but it never went permanently "against the grain," or involved a painful drill and discipline of the inclinations. It was a natural and happy self-expression.

III

It is possible to illustrate Jesus' morality more exactly in relation to some practical problems — family life, the rights of property, reverence for persons, and the treatment of opinion.

(i) Something has already been said as to the attitude which Jesus adopted towards family life.[7] As one who had experienced for thirty years the benefits of a pious hard-working home

---

[1] Mark vi. 34. [2] viii. 2. [3] viii. 22, 23. [4] ix. 36, x. 16.
[5] ix. 50, " Be at peace one with another ".
[6] xi. 25, " Forgive, if ye have aught against any one ".
[7] *Cf.* p. 122.

life, he was willing to sacrifice it all in a moment when the special call of God came. Himself unmarried, he held very strongly the indissoluble nature of the marriage bond. Regarding marriage as a temporary expedient of a transitory world, he was yet noted for his care and reverence for children.

There is, on the whole, a strange lack of stress on family duties and family affections. Once, certainly, Jesus upheld the claim of parents upon the support of their children against the profitable casuistry of the priests: but even then he was more concerned with the irreligion of the Pharisees than with the duty of family affection.[1] More than once he shows special sympathy with the parents of children whom he is asked to cure:[2] and in his forecast of the fall of Jerusalem it is for the mothers that he feels most pity—" Woe unto them that are with child, and to them that give suck in those days!"[3] But, beyond these vague indications of Jesus' attitude, there is nothing. The whole question of family life seems to have been settled, so far as he was concerned, by his great act of renunciation. With that behind, and the speedy end of

[1] Mark vii. 9-13.   [2] v. 40; ix. 21-24.   [3] xiii. 17.

the world in front, a special ethics of the family was well-nigh impossible.

(ii) With regard to private property, Jesus clearly teaches the advisability of its complete surrender.[1] For himself and the disciples this implied the formation of a common fund. When travelling alone, the disciples were told to beg their way from place to place:[2] but when travelling together, they seem to have taken a small stock of provisions—commonly of bread and fish—which, indeed, they were very willing to share with all comers, but which they guarded most thriftily.[3] This custom was no doubt the model of the "communistic" life of the early Church at Jerusalem, until its growth in numbers and complexity made the arrangement impracticable.[4]

Beyond this minimum necessary for common life, property was to be disposed of in charity. Jesus himself did not insist so much upon the method of disposal as the spirit of thoroughness with which it was carried out: he might even prefer "wasting" money to giving it to the poor.[5] But he advised the latter course in at least

---

[1] *Cf.* p. 116. [2] vi. 8.
[3] vi. 38, 43; viii. 5, 8, 14.
[4] Acts ii. 44-45; iv. 32, 34-35. [5] Mark xiv. 4-5.

JESUS' MORALITY

one case,[1] and he always expected of others the charity which he was willing to exercise himself—using one man's colt[2] and another man's room[3] with the splendid simplicity that is possible under Eastern laws of hospitality.

In some cases it may be thought that Jesus showed an actual disregard for the rights of property—though probably here too one is prejudiced by ideas of property derived from Western selfishness and competition.

For instance, the destruction of the swine, which accompanied the healing of the Gerasene demoniac, has been regarded in this light. The exact nature of the incident is very obscure. S. Mark evidently does not regard the destruction of the animals as a mere coincidence, but as a direct result—though not anticipated by Jesus—of the concession made to the evil spirits. We are left with the impression that the thing was an accident, which Jesus could not have foreseen, and that the destruction of property which it involved filled the Gerasenes not with resentment, but with fear. The idea of damage or wrong does not seem to occur either to Jesus or to the bystanders.[4]

A similar issue seems to be raised by the

[1] Mark x. 21. [2] xi. 3. [3] xiv. 14. [4] v. 10-17.

incident of the cleansing of the Temple, which not only shows a splendid scorn of "vested interests" on Jesus' part, but also—if it implies more than a temporary exclusion of the traffickers—must have "spoilt trade" for many licensed hawkers and others. Yet it does not seem to have been so regarded. There is no record of any such hostility as S. Paul roused at Ephesus[1] or Philippi.[2] The explanation of this probably lies in the fact that popular feeling was on Jesus' side in his attack on the officials of the Temple.[3]

Another incident which is sometimes quoted in this connection is the withering of the fig-tree. But there is no reason to suppose that the tree was private property; so that it need not be considered here.

On the whole, the same kind of conclusion seems to be required by the evidence under this head as under the last. Jesus regarded his religious "call" as putting him above the ordinary claims both of family and of property: and he regarded both these things as temporary and transient affairs when compared with the things of the Kingdom of God.

[1] Acts xix. 23-27. [2] Acts xvi. 19.
[3] Mark xi. 15-18.

JESUS' MORALITY

(iii) There is one respect, and that the most important of all, in which Jesus' morality is quite uncompromising. It is that which concerns offences against persons, more particularly by the abuse of personal influence in matters of belief.

There is no parallel in the gospel to the two judgments against this kind of sin which Jesus pronounces. "Whosoever shall cause one of these little ones that believe on me to stumble, it were better for him if a great millstone were hanged about his neck, and he were cast into the sea."[1] Jesus is not thinking so much of the punishment that such sins might deserve, as of the unhappy state of the sinner: he would be better lying already dead and harmless, than he is, still alive, and causing offence to true believers. Again, S. Peter the deserter earns no such rebuke as S. Peter the tempter. "Get thee behind me, Satan," is the answer to his attempt to use his personal influence to dissuade Jesus from a good purpose.[2] And though the offence of Judas was of a rather different kind, it involved so gross an abuse of personal trust and friendship that Jesus could say of him: "Woe unto that man through whom the Son of man is

[1] Mark ix. 42.   [2] viii. 33.

betrayed! Good were it for that man if he had not been born."[1]

Equally stringent is Jesus' advice as to the necessity of destroying any cause of offence in oneself—that is, apparently, any known principle of error, whether in belief or in conduct; any part of the organism whose state may endanger that of the whole.[2]

To Jesus, persons are on quite a different footing from property. Property, in its widest sense, in which it is almost equivalent to "the world," is transient: persons are eternal. It is worth any sacrifice to save "life" whether in oneself or in others. "For what doth it profit a man, to gain the whole world, and forfeit his life? For what should a man give in exchange for his life?"[3]

(iv) Jesus' intense respect for persons was, however, combined with a great zeal for evangelisation. It was a part of his certainty in spiritual affairs never to shrink from imposing his opinion upon others. His work in the world was to catch men's souls—"I will make you to become fishers of men" is the form of his call to the earliest apostles;[4] and again, "I came not to

---

[1] Mark xiv. 21.
[2] ix. 43-47.
[3] viii. 36, 37.
[4] i. 17.

JESUS' MORALITY

call the righteous, but sinners".[1] The primary duty of a disciple is to bear witness, like a lamp that is "brought to be put on the stand";[2] and "there is nothing hid, save that it should be manifested; neither was anything made secret, but that it should come to light".[3]

(v) Jesus, again, was independent of party and personal considerations to a degree that even his enemies remarked, "We know that thou art true, and carest not for any one: for thou regardest not the person of men";[4] and he was willing to show, in his attitude towards fellow-workers who were not disciples, a toleration which his followers found impossible: "There is no man which shall do a mighty work in my name, and be able quickly to speak evil of me. For he that is not against us, is for us."[5]

IV

No attempt to describe Jesus' morality would be at all true that made it no more than an "attitude" or an "opinion". Its great richness lay in positive moral principles, and in the power of enthusiasm that inspired them. Its virtues were frankly, almost fiercely, revolutionary. Its

---

[1] Mark ii. 17. [2] iv. 21; cf. v. 19.
[3] iv. 22. [4] xii. 14. [5] ix. 38-40.

claims convinced the world by their unreasonableness.

There was, for instance, the demand for humility. "Whosoever would become great among you," says Jesus, "shall be your minister,"[1] and, "If any man would be first, he shall be last of all, and minister of all"[2]—a view which Jesus himself admits to go against the whole custom of the world. Indeed the claim amounts to this—that men must become children again in simplicity of innocence and faith: for "Whosoever shall not receive the Kingdom of God as a little child, he shall in no wise enter therein".[3] Jesus himself had so received it.

The demand for self-sacrifice was equally thorough. "If any man would to come after me," says Jesus, "let him deny himself, and take up his cross, and follow me."[4] Discipleship may involve the mutilation of life,[5] the surrender of property and home,[6] and a deep draught of the cup of pain.[7] These things, too, Jesus himself experienced.

But above all else is the only law that Jesus laid down—the law of love. The love of God and the love of one's neighbour are the two great

---

[1] Mark x. 43. [2] ix. 35. [3] x. 15.
[4] viii. 34. [5] ix. 43-47. [6] x. 29. [7] x. 38.

JESUS' MORALITY

commandments. If a man loves God with all his heart and soul and mind and strength, and loves his neighbour as himself, he is, in Jesus' opinion, "not far from the Kingdom of God". That is Jesus' last word in morality.[1]

Jesus' morality did not involve an ascetic holiness. His disciples failed to fast, and were contrasted in this respect with the disciples of John and the Pharisees:[2] of Jesus himself it was said that "he eateth and drinketh with publicans and sinners".[3] Nor did it imply a rigid formalism: Jesus deliberately broke the laws of Sabbath observance,[4] and caused offence by eating with unwashed hands.[5] But it was an entire and enthusiastic self-surrender, springing naturally from a life in which God was the one reality, and all in all.

V

The quality of a man's goodness is best seen by his treatment of sin. What did Jesus think about sin? and how did he treat it?

(i) We have already dealt with what is probably the most important passage of the gospel

---

[1] Mark xii. 28-34. [2] ii. 18. [3] ii. 16.
[4] ii. 23; iii. 5. [5] vii. 2.

for our present purpose—that in which Jesus lays it down that sin is "evil thought"—an inner defilement of a man's heart, which issues in the form of evil deeds.[1] The actual illustrations which he gives of this theory consist of two groups of six kinds of sin. The first group corresponds roughly to the second part of the Mosaic decalogue—"fornications, thefts, murders, adulteries, covetings, wickednesses". These are all put in the plural, as though they represented so many wrong acts. To these are added six more classes put in the singular, as if to represent tendencies or principles of acting, rather than definite acts—"deceit, lasciviousness, an evil eye, railing, pride, and foolishness". Thus even in this classification Jesus seems to go behind the conventional idea that sin means certain bad acts, and to insist on its real nature as "evil thought". Such a view, of course, adds very much to the seriousness of sin.

This, however, is not all. Sin, being in itself evil thought, becomes, in the relations of men to men, evil influence. Personal in origin, it is personal in its effects: and herein, for one who reverenced personality as Jesus did, lies the chief part of its offence. At any cost such sin must

[1] Mark vii. 14-23; cf. p. 141.

be extirpated from one's own life; and any fate is preferable to that of being an "offence" to "one of these little ones". There are here two principles—the first, that persons are sacrosanct; and the second, that personality comes to its perfection rather by self-limitation than by comprehension—by excluding rather than by embracing the opportunity of evil (which is also the opportunity of good). That Jesus inclined to this latter view, rather than to its more popular alternative, can hardly be doubted. His own life illustrated it. But he was able to follow the straight way without sacrificing comprehensiveness, or truth; so that his life becomes a study in the power, not in the weakness, of limitations.[1]

(ii) Serious, however, as is the view which Jesus takes of sin, he never wavers from the certainty that sin can be and generally will be forgiven. The forgiveness of sins is to be a normal subject of prayer, though it is not to be hoped for unless he who prays also forgives.[2] For himself he claims explicitly God's authority (delegated to "the Son of man ... on earth") to forgive sins: and though he regards the power as more honourable and more difficult of use than the power of healing, yet he exercises

[1] Mark ix. 42-47.   [2] xi. 25.

it as readily and spontaneously when the case demands.[1]

Only in one connection is there any mention of a sin which is beyond forgiveness. Certain scribes from Jerusalem had been trying to turn the people against Jesus by accusing him of witchcraft, and attributing his cures to the powers of evil working through him. "Verily I say unto you," is the answer (and the introductory phrase marks the importance of the saying), "All their sins shall be forgiven unto the sons of men, and their blasphemies wherewith soever they shall blaspheme: but whosoever shall blaspheme against the Holy Spirit hath never forgiveness, but is guilty of an eternal sin".[2] This sin was an extreme case of the "railing" or slander mentioned later in Jesus' catalogue of sins:[3] but probably it is implied that any sin becomes unforgivable when it is maliciously and deliberately indulged against God himself, or against the good spirit through which he works in the world. On Jesus' own principles, it cannot be a particular kind of act which is beyond forgiveness, but a certain quality of evil thought.

[1] Mark ii. 1-12.   [2] iii. 28, 29.   [3] vii. 22.

JESUS' MORALITY

And it is through the indulgence of this sin, apparently, that there exists a state alternative to the "eternal life" of the Kingdom of God—a state called "hell," and very inadequately described in such materialistic language as "the unquenchable fire . . . where their worm dieth not, and the fire is not quenched".[1]

VI

In considering Jesus' attitude towards sin, the question must arise, what was his personal experience in respect of sin? The dogma of Jesus' sinlessness is not, of course, stated in the second gospel. If true, it will be established by an examination of the evidence. At any rate such an inquiry should go some way towards clearing up the meaning of a very difficult conception.

(i) The baptism which John preached was a "baptism of repentance unto remission of sins," and those who came to him "were baptised in the river Jordan, confessing their sins". Among them "Jesus came . . . and was baptised of John in the Jordan". The natural inference is that Jesus' baptism was of the ordinary kind, and that

[1] Mark ix. 43-48.

he came to it because he felt the need of "repentance unto remission of sins".[1]

Remembering in how many respects Jesus shared the moral and religious ideas of his contemporaries, we shall hardly be surprised at this. The absence of penitence—an essential part of the religious spirit, and one which deepens in direct proportion to goodness—would have been far more difficult to understand. Moreover, the second gospel probably implies that the new life of the Spirit, with its power to heal, and its authority to teach, began at the time of Jesus' baptism. Would there not be at the same time some ending of the old life, some inward change corresponding to the outward renunciation of family and friends?

There is perhaps some evidence that the passage was interpreted as above, in its natural sense, in S. Matthew's attempt to get over the difficulty of it—"Then cometh Jesus from Galilee to the Jordan unto John, to be baptised of him. But John would have hindered him, saying, I have need to be baptised of thee, and comest thou to me? But Jesus answering said unto him, Suffer it now: for thus it becometh us to fulfil all righteousness. Then he suffereth him."[2]

[1] Mark i. 9. [2] Matt. iii. 13-15.

JESUS' MORALITY

There is no support for this interpolation. It is not mentioned, for instance, by S. Luke, though it refers (in its contrast of the two baptisms) to words which occur in S. Luke as well as in S. Matthew. It reads too much like an editorial after-thought. In any case it gives no motive for Jesus' coming to the baptism so natural or adequate as that suggested by S. Mark. It seems, then, that the idea of sinlessness must somehow include the experience of repentance. How this is possible is perhaps hinted by the penitence of Christian saints. But any real solutions of the difficulty in Jesus' case must depend upon evidence yet to be considered.

(ii) "And as he was going forth into the way, there ran one to him, and kneeled to him, and asked him, Good Master, what shall I do that I may inherit eternal life? And Jesus said unto him, why callest thou me good? none is good save one, even God." The stress in the last sentence is on "good," not on "me": but this hardly lessens the force of the passage. It is not enough to suggest that the young man's idea of goodness needed correction, and that Jesus would point him from a wrong to a right meaning of the word. Nor is it Jesus' intention to deny, as man, any equality with God. The address "Good Master" contained no such suggestion. Theology is out of place in this passage, which deals with plain words in a plain way. There is, in fact, no adequate alternative to the natural interpretation. Jesus did not think himself "good" in the sense in which the young man had used the word, and in the sense in which it would be commonly used of God.[1]

S. Matthew, as in the last passage, so here, makes what can only be called a clumsy attempt to get rid of what seemed to him to be a difficulty; for, in place of "Good Master, what shall I do . . .?" he has "Master, what good thing shall I do . . .?" and in place of "why callest thou me good . . .?" he writes, "why askest thou me concerning that which is good?"[2] The attempt to rewrite the passage—if that is what has been done—is evidence to the effect that the literal interpretation of it is the most natural one.

In any case this would seem to follow from the last section. If Jesus could feel that he needed to undergo the baptism of repentance, he could and would also disclaim divine perfection. And this, again, agrees with the idea of the gradual growth of Jesus' Messianic consciousness. If he did not at this time feel himself to

[1] Mark x. 17, 18. [2] Matt. xix. 16, 17.

JESUS' MORALITY

be good in the sense in which God is good, neither did he think himself to be divine, in the sense in which God is divine.

(iii) There is one other passage that may be thought to bear on the same question. The story of the withering of the fig-tree, as given in the second Gospel, suggests no motive for the miracle but the natural one of disappointment at the failure of the fruit. Further, it gives support to this by its definite placing of the miracle. It occurs on the morning after the first day in Jerusalem, when Jesus, sad and angry at the desecration of the Temple, has made up his mind to take the law into his own hands, and to drive out the traffickers. From Jesus' hunger thus early in the morning we are left to infer that he had spent the night fasting, and on the open hillside.[1] The only suggested motive lies in the weakness of the flesh.

S. Luke omits the incident altogether, though from the form of another passage it seems likely that he knew it.[2] S. Matthew heightens the miracle by making the tree wither instantaneously, but only succeeds in obscuring the motive of the act.[3]

---

[1] Mark xi. 12-14. [2] Luke xvii. 5, 6 ; *cf.* xiii. 6-9—a parable about a fig-tree, from which, it has been suggested, the story of the miracle may have been derived.
[3] Matt. xxi. 18-22.

All that we can safely say is that the second gospel seems to have handed on a true account of an act of Jesus from an age which found no difficulty in it to one that did. The act, whatever its exact motive, was not inconsistent with S. Mark's (and that implies, probably, S. Peter's) idea of Jesus. If it is difficult for us to reconcile it with the nature of the Incarnate, is it because we understand him better, or worse, than they did?

The truth seems to be, that S. Mark's Gospel reproduces the beliefs of an age which had not yet become theological, and which was therefore not in a position to feel the theoretical difficulty of facts which experience and tradition recorded. More than this—it was not merely untheological: it had personal memory of Jesus. And just as the inconsistencies of great men are not so apparent to their contemporaries as to later generations, who have lost the unifying medium of personal experience; so to the first generation of Christians there not only seemed to be, but there really was perfect consistency between the claims and the characteristics of the Incarnate.

Can we, however, recover the ground of that consistency, so far as the present topic is concerned? Can we say what there was in the experience and teaching of Jesus that enabled the Church to believe such things (as we have been considering) of him whom it worshipped as the Christ, the Son of God? The experience of repentance, the disclaiming of "goodness," the weakness of the flesh—are not all these features in the Incarnation to be explained by one great fact, —Jesus' consciousness of the reality of temptation? If what we have already said on this subject be true,[1]—if Jesus' whole life involved a real contest with temptation, and if he knew that his nature included the possibility of that "evil thought" which was the source of sin— then some reason, at least, is given for experiences which would otherwise be inexplicable. "For we have not a high priest that cannot be touched with the feeling of our infirmities; but One that hath been in all points tempted like as we are, yet without sin."[2]

Whether this be the true interpretation or not, the facts, if facts they be, must not be ignored, or explained away; on the contrary no doctrine of the Incarnation can be considered as adequate which is not able to include them.

[1] *Cf.* p. 142.   [2] Heb. iv. 15.

CHAPTER VII

JESUS' RELIGION

I

AS no strict line can be drawn between Jesus' morality and his religion, but the latter is a particular expression of the former, so there will be no real division between Jesus' religion and Jesus himself, but his religion will be the natural expression of his self-consciousness. That is to say, we are now very close to the highest and hardest inquiry of all—What did Jesus know of himself? Who did he think himself to be? Yet, as before, it is possible, for practical purposes, to isolate certain parts of the evidence, and to deal with them under the present head.

It is simply and solely on grounds of religion that Jesus makes his claim upon the world. Not as a political deliverer: he refused the popular Messiahship, and chose the death of the cross. Not as a social reformer: he looked not for the regeneration of the old society, but for the inauguration of a new. Not as a moralist or philosopher : he knew no morality or philosophy apart from the love of God, and of man through God. Not as a cultured man of the world : his way was to sacrifice faculties, rather than to sanctify them. Like a man on his death-bed, who feels that everything is slipping away from him but the need of God, so Jesus lives in the world. Nothing in this life, he feels, can last, unless it is rooted in the future life. Nothing matters for man, except God. No study, no motive, no standard, no value is worth consideration which is not simply and solely religious.

Moreover, Jesus claims to be himself the guide and authority in religion. He accepts quite naturally the position which the disciples give him. His words and way of life are a true revelation of God, a certain though "strait" gate of the kingdom of God. The study of his life and death ought to move all men to the conviction that "this was the Son of God".

II

The conditions of Jesus' early life cannot but have had a great influence upon his religion.

Yet we can do no more than suggest certain directions that this influence must have taken, on the basis of evidence which is sometimes negative and generally indirect.

(i) As regards influences of home, and class, and nationality, Jesus shared the Jewish worship of the One God, the Jewish zeal for holiness, the Jewish patriotism. As a Galilean he was brought up in the provincial simplicity and piety for which the lake-country was so remarkable. As a carpenter of Nazareth, he inherited an active, working faith, one that faced the hard facts and cramping circumstances of life.

(ii) Jesus' "Churchmanship" was not merely that of his contemporaries. There was, doubtless, a genuine dislike among Galileans of the formalism and official pretensions of the religious sects. But Jesus, whilst sharing, we may suppose, in the daily observances of household piety, made distrust and dislike of formalism a ruling principle of his religion. Attending—as seems probable — the village synagogue every Sabbath day, he yet became a convinced nonconformist with regard to some of the commonest practices of religion. Sharing the general reverence for Jerusalem with its Temple and its festivals, he could never think of it except with the foreboding of its fall. The real current of his religion flowed deep below the outward forms of Jewish Churchmanship.

(iii) Jesus' intense belief in the power of prayer, his knowledge and treatment of the Scriptures, his zeal for works of charity, all have their roots in the family life and village companionship. The religious needs of fishermen and carpenters, the lovable unlovely lives of "publicans and sinners," the hypocritical righteousness of religious officials—all came into his early experience, and contributed something to his religious outlook. Then came the Baptist's preaching, and fused all this raw material of religion into a white-hot love of God and man.

III

What forms did it take?—forms, that is, definitely religious, not merely moral—main heads of religious principles and practice? Two pre-eminently—humility and faith.

(i) Jesus' humility was based, as all genuine humility is, on a sense of the reality of sin. One need not have sinned, to be humbled by sin: to have been tempted is to have seen sin face to face, and to have found oneself, apart from God, powerless. So Jesus knows that his flesh is weak, that he is not divinely "good".

And this experience became a way of life, in which self-will habitually submitted to the law of God, and to the need of man. "Not what I will, but what thou wilt," was Jesus' permanent attitude towards God. The obedient service and voluntary humility of the disciples was based upon the personal example of one who "came not to be ministered unto, but to minister, and to give his life a ransom for many".

Again, though Jesus had no hesitation in imposing his opinion as dogma, or his morality as law: though he never wavered in the certainty of his faith in God, yet he seems to have shrunk from self-expression in personal affairs. His reserve in matters of religion is shown by his choice of no more than twelve apostles, to whom alone "the mystery of the Kingdom of God" was revealed; and in the exclusion of all but three, even of these, from the scenes of his most important miracles, his moments of ecstasy, or his prayers; whilst even the privileged three can only pray apart from him at the time of supreme temptation in the

Garden of Gethsemane.[1] Jesus did not care to talk about his "religious experiences". The story of the baptism and temptation is the only part of the gospel which seems to be told by himself. The only exception to this rule of reserve is in the repeated prophecies of the Passion and Second Coming of the Son of man.

There is, indeed, a splendid disregard of those subjective feelings and "attitudes" which are often the caricature of genuine religious experience. Religion is not a matter of opinion, a "question" of any kind, an "interest" that may or may not appeal. It is objective, simple, unquestionable. It does not matter how one feels as the result of living for God, or whether it is reasonable to die for him: true humility is to live and die, asking no questions.

(ii) Faith has been so variously defined that it becomes of extreme importance to know what Jesus meant by it. Or, more strictly, we should ask what there was in the religion of Jesus which the Church came to call faith.

It was, first, an entire trust in God's presence with him and care for him. Jesus could quite simply disregard physical dangers, or the fear of

[1] Mark xiv. 32-35; notice the three stages of privacy—the eight disciples, the three, Jesus himself.

death, through the power of faith. Once it is recorded that he slept peacefully in a small boat during a severe storm. It was faith as well as weariness which enabled him to sleep so ; and it was faith which made him rebuke the disciples, not for doubting his ability to still the storm, but for fearing lest the boat should sink. To himself such an event was unthinkable.[1] One remembers the very similar story related of Julius Cæsar. But what in Cæsar was perhaps a pose, was in Jesus quite natural and spontaneous.

On another occasion Jesus rebuked his disciples, in similar strain, for doubting his ability to provide enough food for a journey.[2] It is not suggested that Jesus deliberately neglected the ordinary precautions ; indeed, it is stated that a common stock of food, however small, was generally maintained ; and the miracles of feeding are expressly recorded as exceptional. But it is implied that Jesus did not rely upon such provision, and thought it as impossible that he should starve as that he should drown. Moreover he extends this personal faith to his apostles, when he sends them out to preach with no provision for their journey.[3]

[1] Mark iv. 35-41.   [2] viii. 17-21.   [3] vi. 8.

JESUS' RELIGION

Secondly, faith is power. It is through faith that Jesus works many of his cures: faith on the part of the patient is sometimes, though not generally, a necessary condition of the exercise of the healing power.

The disciples are called a "faithless generation" because they cannot cast out an evil spirit (it is a specially severe case; and it is implied that their faith had been sufficient for less serious demands). "All things," says Jesus, "are possible to him that believeth;" and though in this case prayer is the special means of cure, yet faith is its ground.[1] Again, to those who "have faith in God" nothing is impossible—no physical "miracle," and (which is more wonderful) no spiritual achievement. This faith is akin to prayer—"All things whatsoever ye pray and ask for, believe that ye have received them, and ye shall have them".[2] Like all faith, it is an intense persuasion of identity of will with God: God is with me, on my side, meets my every need, is all in all to me: to believe that one has, is to have; to believe that one is, is to be. If it be objected that such an attitude could only lead to disillusionment, the answer is, that in Jesus' case, at least, it did not. It seems to be

---

[1] Mark ix. 19, 23, 29.   [2] xi. 22-24.

literally true that a faith which is strong enough can defy disillusionment.

Jesus' faith generally asks for an answer in those who are its beneficiaries. "If thou *wilt*, thou *canst* make me clean" is a patient's summary of Jesus' ordinary demand for faith in cases of healing.[1] Often (perhaps generally) the mere request created in him the "will" to cure. A special degree of faith might call out a special benefit, such as the forgiveness of sins,[2] or turn his unwillingness into willingness.[3] Absence of faith in one case at least made it impossible for him to work cures with his usual freedom.[4] In some cases he asked for proof of faith before doing anything.[5] In others, the sufferer's faith could make him work a cure "automatically"—not indeed without his knowledge, but without his will.[6]

Thirdly, Jesus' faith was not merely a gratitude for past mercies and a trust in present support, but also a strong hope in a future event. He believed it impossible for himself to drown or starve, not simply because God was with him, but because God was keeping him for a special work, designing his life and

[1] Mark i. 40.   [2] ii. 5.   [3] vii. 29.
[4] vi. 5.   [5] ix. 23.   [6] v. 29.

death in view of a great future end. The faith in which he found power, and taught that others could find it, was the partial exercise, in this present world, of a faculty meant for the Kingdom of God. It was in faith that he saw the spiritual world as the real world, and the present as a veil upon the face of the future. Jesus' voluntary death was the crucial experiment designed by faith to solve the mystery of his existence.

So Jesus' faith answers to his humility, the certainty to the reserve, the closeness to the distance of God. The inconsistency of the two things is superficial. They are complementary parts of the essence of Jesus' religious experience.

IV

Faith and humility, the essence of Jesus' religion, necessarily grew up under, and adapted themselves to a particular religious organisation. It is impossible to study them quite apart from Jesus' relation to the Jewish Church.

For thirty years, so far as we can ascertain, Jesus conformed to the ordinary requirements of his national religion. We gather that this was so from the absence of any contrary evidence with regard to the early life at Nazareth. We infer it from the absence of any reproach on the part of Jesus' opponents. We see clear signs of it in his own acts in later life—in the custom of beginning his preaching in the local synagogues,[1] in his orthodox observance of the Passover, in his zeal for the orderly worship of the Temple,[2] and in his instructions to the cleansed leper to carry out the requirements of the Mosaic law.[3]

But this general conformity was not inconsistent, in Jesus' mind, with definite opposition to some specific cases of formalism, with which the national religion had become identified, and with which it needed a bold man to quarrel. From an early period in his ministry Jesus gave up the religious observance of fasting, or at least did not require it of his disciples: and when taxed with this he defended himself on the general principle that a new spirit of religion cannot be satisfied with the old forms, but demands new. The old formalities did not require too much; they required too little, and must break down under the strain of a new and more exacting

[1] Mark i. 21; vi. 2. This seems to have been Jesus' regular practice, until after the rejection at Nazareth.
[2] xi. 17.   [3] i. 44.

spirit.[1] In the same way Jesus deliberately broke the ordinary rules of Sabbath observance, with the plea that God is best satisfied by the satisfaction of human needs, and that "the Sabbath was made for man, not man for the Sabbath".[2] Similarly with the custom of washing before meat, where Jesus passes from specific to general denunciation,[3] or with the ecclesiastical fiction of "Corban," by which, again, a supposed religious duty was allowed to override a plain human need.[4]

Jesus' nonconformity, as we can see from these cases, was his way of reasserting real religion—that genuine love and service of God which finds its normal expression through the love and service of man—against a detached and abstract worship. Religion in every age must make some such protest against what passes for religion. It was not so much the extreme "formality" of Judaism as the unique sanity of Jesus' religion, which heaped special denunciation upon the Pharisees and scribes.

What, however, was Jesus' relation, more specifically, to the religious "parties" of his time? It is as much a mistake to think that

[1] Mark ii. 18-22. [2] ii. 23-28; iii. 1-4.
[3] vii. 1-8. [4] vii. 9-13.

he quarrelled equally with them all, as to ignore the fact that he found himself out of sympathy with most of those who, on the whole, adequately represented the purest religion of ancient times.

The condemnation and death of Jesus were organised by "the chief priests and the scribes and the elders".[1] But of these it is the priests who are singled out as the leaders of the attack, the most active and bitter opponents. It was the chief priests who bargained with the traitor,[2] who "accused" Jesus "of many things" before Pilate,[3] who "for envy delivered him up,"[4] who "stirred up the multitudes" to ask for the release of Barabbas,[5] and who, with the scribes, mocked at Jesus as he hung upon the cross.[6] Yet Jesus never seems to have spoken against them as he spoke against the scribes. He respected their office, if not their character: the cleansed leper is told to "show himself to the priest," and carry out the customary formalities of the law:[7] and it is regarded as right that

---

[1] This grouping of titles occurs once in Jesus' prophecies of his passion (viii. 31), and four times in the course of the last chapters of the gospel; without the "elders," four times more; with "the council" twice.

[2] Mark xiv. 10.   [3] xv. 3.   [4] xv. 10.
[5] xv. 11.   [6] xv. 31.   [7] i. 44.

JESUS' RELIGION

only the priests should be privileged to eat the shewbread in the Temple.[1] Probably Jesus regarded the opposition of the priests as official rather than personal. Certainly it was an inevitable result of the publication of the Messianic claims in Jerusalem; and Jesus expected, if he did not intend, to rouse it, when he entered on the last week of his ministry. The scribes, he felt, were misleading the people as to the character of the Messiah: the Pharisees were obscuring the laws of God by their "tradition": the priests as such were not to blame for their zealous service of a God whom they misunderstood.

It was the scribes who were Jesus' most active enemies, and whom he most plainly condemned. Whereas the priests' opposition was excited by Jesus' presence in Jerusalem, the scribes "came down from Jerusalem" to Galilee for the express purpose of thwarting and discrediting Jesus' mission.[2] They it was who accused him of blasphemy when he claimed to forgive sins,[3] who objected to his eating "with publicans and sinners,"[4] and whom he found "questioning with the disciples" when he came down from the

[1] Mark ii. 26. [2] iii. 22.
[3] ii. 6, 7.   [4] ii. 16.

Transfiguration.[1] They alone are charged with the "eternal sin" which "hath never forgiveness," because they attribute the works of the Holy Spirit in Jesus to the agency of Beelzebub, "the prince of the devils".[2] And so it is the scribes who earn Jesus' most outspoken condemnation for pride, dishonesty, and hypocrisy. "Beware of the scribes," he says, "which desire to walk in long robes, and to have salutations in the marketplaces, and chief seats in the synagogues, and chief places at feasts: they which devour widows' houses, and for a pretence make long prayers; these shall receive greater condemnation."[3] Yet even these men, in so far as they are merely mistaken, and not malevolent, may be argued with: Jesus twice treats them so.[4] And there is one good scribe whose discreetness and piety move Jesus to the commendation, "Thou art not far from the Kingdom of God".[5]

Between Jesus and the Pharisees one feels that there is less open hostility, but a more complete absence of sympathy. Only the Pharisees are described (and it can hardly be an acci-

---

[1] Mark ix. 14.   [2] iii. 22, 28-30.
[3] xii. 38-40.   [4] ix. 11-13; xii. 35-37.
[5] xii. 20-34.

dent) as "tempting" Jesus.¹ Theirs is a subtle influence for bad, fitly comparable to leaven.² No good Pharisee is mentioned, and no redeeming feature of Pharisaism. The sect represented the spirit of formalism which was the very antithesis of Jesus' religion: it was too intangible to denounce, as the scribes were denounced: but Jesus' whole life and teaching were a protest against it.

The Sadducees, as a small and select party, do not seem to have joined as such in the ordinary attacks upon Jesus, though many of them did so as priests. They are only once mentioned in this gospel, and that in connection with a rather ridiculous question respecting the future life, which was always a stumbling-block to them. From the tone of Jesus' answer it is clear that he is more sorry than angry at their ignorance, and would suggest to them a truer view of the meaning of life beyond the grave.³

Jesus' attitude towards the religious sects completely bears out the character for independence and integrity that even his enemies con-

---

[1] Mark viii. 11, x. 2; and the same idea seems to be implied by xii. 13.
[2] viii. 15.   [3] xii. 18-27.

ceded to him. "Master," they said, "we know that thou art true, and carest not for any one: for thou regardest not the person of men, but of a truth teachest the way of God."[1] He was able, that is, to stand outside not only all parties, but also all the lower motives and judgements that go to the making of parties. His one care being for God, and his one concern to teach the way of God, he could judge all religious pretensions by the highest possible standard, without misgiving and without pride. Indeed his "relation" to this party or that was not an attitude consciously taken up, but an instinctive like or dislike for the type of character represented by the particular sect.

V

Something must here be said, though not in such a way as to prejudice the final discussion of Jesus' self-knowledge, about the relation in which Jesus stood to the Messianic beliefs of his countrymen.

During his early years he doubtless shared those beliefs, and became familiar with the language which was afterwards his natural expression of them. But there is no evidence in the

[1] Mark xii. 14.

JESUS' RELIGION

second gospel (indeed there is a considerable presumption to the contrary) that at that time he identified them in any special way with himself. The spiritual awakening that came to him through the Baptist's message, and the wonderful experience at the moment of his baptism, are represented as the beginning of Jesus' conscious Messiahship.

From that point onwards his relation to the Messianic beliefs seems to have passed through three fairly well-defined stages. The first extends from the time of the first preaching down to the journey into the villages of Cæsarea Philippi. During this period Jesus was constantly recognised and acknowledged in Messianic language by the victims of "possession":[1] but he always refused such homage, and did his best to secure the silence of those who knew him and the ignorance of those who did not. Once only, and that in what may be a detached saying, here misplaced, he calls himself the "Son of man".[2] When we come across any indication of the opinions which were held about him, it is to find that his disciples did not know what to think of him,[3] that his relations and

[1] Mark i. 24 (marginal reading), 34; iii. 11; v. 7.
[2] ii. 28.   [3] iv. 41, "Who then is this . . . ?"

friends regarded him as "the carpenter,"[1] that Herod supposed him to be John the Baptist come to life again,[2] and that to the common people he was Elijah, or "one of the prophets".[3] He was not yet identified with the Messiah. For himself, he preferred the title "prophet";[4] and that may be taken as the best summary of his claims during this first period.

A new stage begins with the journey to the villages of Cæsarea Philippi. Partly because he is now free from the publicity of Galilee, and the fear of political complications, partly because the question has by this time become a pressing one for himself, he asks the disciples (it is implied, for the first time) what is their opinion of him. He expects more than a repetition of the popular superstitions. But it is regarded as a new and perhaps dangerous admission when S. Peter answers: "Thou art the Christ," that is, the Messiah. This claim had been kept, and was still to be kept, a profound secret, discoverable only by the insight of habitual companionship.[5] The same privacy is preserved in the Transfiguration, immediately after; and in the conversation which follows it

[1] Mark vi. 3.   [2] vi. 14, 16.   [3] vi. 15.
[4] vi. 4.   [5] viii. 29, 30.

the conviction that the Baptist was Elijah is also regarded as a new one, not hitherto made known to the disciples.[1] But from this moment the use of the title "Son of man" becomes common in Jesus' talks with his disciples, and they are told repeatedly of the nature of the Messiahship —the crisis of rejection and death through which he must pass into his spiritual Kingdom.[2] At the same time we get evidence of the way in which the disciples understood this new teaching from the request of S. James and S. John (two of the three who were present at the Transfiguration) to be allowed a special place in the Kingdom.[3]

At the end of this second stage occurs a saying which marks the transition to the third and last period in the relationship that we are considering. "The Son of man," says Jesus, using his favourite Messianic title, "came not to be ministered unto, but to minister, and to give his life a ransom for many."[4] It is not only that Jesus comes to regard his death as having a social as well as a personal significance: it is also that the centre of interest shifts more and more to himself, his own passion and death, as the supreme act of one who now openly claims

[1] Mark ix. 11-13.   [2] viii. 31; ix. 9, 31; x. 33.
[3] x. 35-40.   [4] x. 45.

to be the Messiah. For now Jesus, who had refused the acknowledgments of "devils," invites the Hosannas of the crowd.[1] Questioned as to his authority, he claims that it stands or falls with that of the Baptist.[2] In the parable of the Vineyard he is God's son and heir, greater than all the prophets.[3] Though no son of David, he may yet be the Messiah.[4] He applies to himself the eschatological and Messianic language of the book of Daniel.[5] To the high priest's question, "Art thou the Christ, the Son of the Blessed?" he answers simply, "I am".[6]

It seems, then, that Jesus only gradually developed his Messianic consciousness, and only gradually revealed it to the disciples; that to most people he remained throughout "the prophet" or "the Nazarene"; and that his claim to be the Messiah, although more openly stated in the last week's preaching, seemed sufficiently novel and outrageous to those who condemned him. Doubtless, the underlying cause both of the reserve with which Jesus treated his claims and of the opposition which, when stated, they aroused, was "the mystery of the Kingdom"—that new interpretation of the Messiahship which was so certain

[1] Mark xi. 10.   [2] xi. 27-33.   [3] xii. 1-12.
[4] xii. 35-37.   [5] xiii. 26.   [6] xiv. 61, 62.

JESUS' RELIGION

and central in Jesus' faith, and so unintelligible to his contemporaries.

VI

Jesus was not a theologian. But there are two respects in which it becomes necessary to attempt some statement of his theological belief, in any sketch of his religious position. One is with regard to the Holy Spirit : the other is in respect of God.

In dealing with the doctrine of the Holy Spirit, so far as anything can be gathered about it from the second gospel, we shall try carefully to distinguish evidence for Jesus' own beliefs from the possible accretion of later ideas. It is difficult to believe, for instance, that the Baptist's prophecy of Jesus' gift of the Holy Ghost, contrasted with his own "baptism of water," is unaffected by later knowledge. At any rate, " John's baptism " was undergone in later years by some who " did not so much as hear whether the Holy Ghost was given " : and it is not unlikely that John's message would become adapted to the experience of the early Church.[1]

But there are sufficient indications, apart from any such doubts, as to what Jesus himself be-

[1] Mark i. 8 ; *cf.* Acts xix. 1-4.

lieved. Thus in the narrative of his baptism it is stated, apparently upon his own authority (for the vision was for himself alone) that "he saw the heavens rent asunder, and the Spirit as a dove descending upon him".[1] The comparison to a dove is a conventional one in the Old Testament: Jesus expressed in this form the new experience which came to him at this moment—the certainty of his "call," and of the gift of the Spirit of God, for healing and teaching and the "prophetic" life. So, immediately afterwards, it is the Spirit which "driveth him forth into the wilderness" for the temptation[2]—the testing of the vocation which has just been given to him. It is the good or holy Spirit in himself which gives him power over the spirits of evil: hence the seriousness of the sin which he calls "blasphemy against the Holy Spirit,"—when men attribute to an evil spirit the obvious work of the good Spirit.[3] The Spirit which so works through him is the same Spirit as that which inspired David,[4] and the prophets of old: and it will still be given in the future, to help the disciples in their witness to the world—"it is not ye that speak, but the Holy Ghost".[5]

[1] Mark i. 10. [2] i. 12. [3] iii. 22-30.
[4] xii. 36. [5] xiii. 11.

It cannot be said that in any of these passages the Spirit is regarded as a person, in any proper sense of the word. Yet it is described as corresponding, in its powers and forms of manifestation, to the " evil spirits " : it has a special understanding with them, being able to recognise and be recognised by them : its special powers are called out by the presence of such spirits, who " believe and tremble " because their time of mastery is at an end. One may almost say that religious enthusiasm, such as that of Jesus, was a kind of "possession" by a good spirit, in nature not unlike those other cases of " possession," though in results so very different. It has, for instance, its own physical phenomena, such as the " power proceeding from him " which Jesus was sometimes conscious of expending,[1] and which could work cures without his will, or by the simple contact of his clothes.[2] It is possible, though it cannot be assumed, that Jesus regarded his " spirit "—that part of him which was willing when the flesh was weak,[3] and that faculty which enabled him to read men's minds and hearts,[4]—as the seat of this indwelling Holy Spirit. At any rate the latter was not, so to speak, an

[1] Mark v. 30.   [2] v. 28, 29 ; vi. 56.
[3] xiv. 38.   [4] ii. 8.

original part of himself, but something in itself permanent, divine, coming into men for temporal purposes from outside; manifesting itself almost as a kind of stuff or nerve-force in the body, but being in reality the good Spirit, the actual power and inspiration of God.

VII

What a man is may be judged infallibly from what he believes about God. We are therefore upon the edge of the most difficult and hazardous task of all, when we raise this latter question with respect to Jesus. And yet it is the necessary completion of our plan; and if we were to draw back here, we should condemn all that has gone before. For if the inductive or scientific method is at all applicable, and if we have been right in trying to interpret the Gospel empirically until we should find any point in which that method broke down, then, in proportion to our success hitherto, we shall hope for success throughout, and trust the tried weapons in a larger venture.

Of the meaning of the phrase "the Kingdom of God," which was constantly upon Jesus' lips, we have no further need to speak in detail.

Sufficient has already been said about it.[1] We need only recall the general fact that the Kingdom, which belongs to another life and another world, is regarded as more real and important than the present life and the kingdoms of this world. This of course rests upon the belief that God, to whom the Kingdom belongs, finds his true being, and, if we may so say, his most absorbing interests outside the present order of things. To have this belief is not necessarily to disbelieve in the constant presence of God in this world. But it does seem commonly to carry with it that tinge of dualism from which few religious enthusiasts have been wholly free. The mind which cannot conceive God as finding his chief interest in the present life, and filling every part of it with his presence, is apt to hand over the empty spaces to the dominion of the Devil. Such, indeed, we have seen some reason to suppose, was the form of Jesus' thought on this subject.[2] We therefore come to the study of Jesus' belief about God with this general presupposition of a dual government of the present life, side by side with a solitary transcendence of God in a future life, and in a world that stands behind the veil of present things.

[1] Chap. v., § viii.   [2] Chap. iv., § v.

Among the very great number of mentions of the name or attributes of God in the second gospel, we shall confine ourselves to those which occur in words actually attributed to Jesus. Even so we shall find that there are between twenty and thirty passages which bear directly upon the question, and cannot be ignored. Yet they fall fairly easily into four classes, and can best be considered in that form. Some of the sayings in which the name of God occurs, or which refer directly to him, may be said to embody the conventional language of Jewish religion: some deal with the relation of God to man: others with the relation of God to Jesus himself: whilst a fourth class involve direct teaching about the nature of God.

(i) Under the head of conventional religious language one may fairly class such phrases as "the house of God,"[1] "the will of God,"[2] "the commandment of God,"[3] "the word of God,"[4] "the power of God,"[5] and "the beginning of the creation which God created".[6] This language was then, as it is now, the current coinage of religion; Jesus used it, we may presume, in the sense in which other teachers used it, and in which his

---

[1] Mark ii. 26.   [2] iii. 35.   [3] vii. 8, 9.
[4] vii. 13.   [5] xii. 24.   [6] xiii. 19.

audience would understand it. The last phrase is indeed an echo of the words of Jewish Scripture, and may be taken as an instance of the fidelity with which S. Mark seems to have reproduced the fashion of Jesus' ordinary speech. Moreover, the preponderance of thought throughout is towards the thoroughly Jewish idea of an active, forceful, severe God, who lays down rules and expects to see them obeyed. The familiarity of the language should not blind us to this habit of thought to which it most fitly belongs, and which Jesus, as a Jew, shared with his fellow-countrymen.

(ii) In harmony with these ideas is the sense of those sayings which deal with the relations between God and man. It is not the closeness of God and man, but their separateness, which is most emphasised. The "things of God" and the "things of men" are two mutually exclusive classes.[1] Divine and human agency are upon different planes,[2] and what is impossible upon the one plane is easily conceivable upon the other.[3] We have a duty to the rulers of this world, and we have a duty to God: they are not the same duty.[4] How much weight can be

[1] Mark viii. 33.
[2] x. 9.
[3] x. 27.
[4] xii. 17; cf. p. 119.

attached to this last passage, is a question which has already been discussed. But it certainly appears that Jesus would have had little sympathy either with a philosophy that emphasises the immanence at the expense of the transcendence of God, or with a way of thinking and speaking about religion that claims a kind of personal intimacy between God and man. This is only one instance of many which might be suggested in which much of the language of Christian devotion would be inconceivable in the mouth of Christ.

(iii) We proceed to examine Jesus' sayings about God, with a view to determining the relationship in which he considered himself to stand towards God. In the first place we may say generally that there is nothing in these sayings, so far as they are reported (that is to say, according to our hypothesis, adequately reported) in the second gospel, inconsistent with the view that Jesus' attitude towards God was in the main that of his countrymen — an attitude in which God's word was to be fulfilled, God's commandments to be kept, God's will to be done in earth, as in heaven ; a life whose highest function was to " have faith in God ".[1]

[1] Mark xi. 22.

Looking a little more closely at what was involved in this separateness between Jesus and God, and isolating it for the moment from some considerations which must afterwards be taken into account, we find at least three respects in which Jesus is conscious, if we may so put it, of his distance from God. Morally, the same language cannot be used of his goodness as of God's:[1] intellectually, there is knowledge in the Father's mind which is withheld from the Son:[2] and in practical conduct there is a duality, if not an opposition, of wills, which involves a conscious and genuine struggle against temptation.[3] These are all important points, which have often been insisted upon. Have we anything to set on the other side? Under the head of morality, it cannot be said that there is any passage in this gospel in which Jesus draws any special attention to his own morality, much less puts it on a level with God's. Amongst all the claims that he makes, this never finds a place. He calls men to follow him, not to admire him; not to imitate, but to serve. His own aim is to live for God, and to die for men.

[1] Mark x. 18; cf. p. 159.
[2] xiii. 32; cf. p. 100.
[3] xiv. 36; cf. p. 143.

Intellectually, however, it may be said that there is other evidence. Side by side with the acknowledgment of ignorance already mentioned, there is a claim to know God's plans in certain respects.

The privilege of sitting on Jesus' right and left hand in his glory " is for them for whom it hath been prepared ".[1] The parable of the Vineyard gives in figurative form an outline of God's scheme for the redemption of the Jewish nation.[2] Of the coming days of tribulation it is said that, " Except the Lord had shortened the days, no flesh would have been saved : but for the elect's sake, whom he chose, he shortened the days ".[3] These passages may fairly be taken (together with some others, which are not strictly in place here) to show that Jesus did speak as though he had some special knowledge of the counsels of God. And yet it may be doubted whether the proper analogy to this may not be the prophetic power which was commonly experienced by early Christians.[4]

Again, as regards the relationship which one would naturally suppose to be the ground of such knowledge, we know that Jesus regarded

---

[1] Mark x. 40.   [2] xii. 1-9.   [3] xiii. 20.
[4] *e.g.* Acts xi. 28 ; xxi. 11 ; xxvii. 10, 22-26, 31.

JESUS' RELIGION

himself not merely as sent by God, but as in some special sense God's representative: "Whosoever receiveth me, receiveth not me, but him that sent me".[1] And the same idea is in his mind when he bids the man whom he has healed go home and tell his friends how great things the Lord (that is God, not Jesus) has done for him, and how he had mercy on him.[2] To this relationship of representation is attached in some cases the terminology of "Father" and "Son". But in two of the passages that might be quoted in this sense the language is derived from the Old Testament,[3] and in a third it is figurative;[4] whilst the private prayer, "Abba, Father,"[5] must be taken in connection with that other case in which the sonship is shared with the whole body of disciples—"Whensoever ye stand praying, forgive, if ye have aught against any one; that your Father also which is in heaven may forgive you your trespasses".[6] There may be more to say about this point at a later stage: provisionally one may point out how little evidence there is that Jesus himself attached special meaning to the names Father and Son in this connection. But that God

[1] Mark ix. 37.   [2] v. 19.   [3] viii. 38; xiv. 61, 62.
[4] xii. 1-9.   [5] xiv. 36.   [6] xi. 25.

was very real and present to him, and that to be shaken in the faith of God's love was the sorest trial that could be undergone, is abundantly proved by the last cry, a cry of despair, from the Cross—"My God, my God, why hast thou forsaken me?"[1]

(iv) The God in whom Jesus believes is good, powerful, alive, and one. His goodness determines the meaning of the word "good," and monopolises the use of it.[2] There is no limit to his power—"all things are possible with God,"[3] in the future life no less than in the present.[4] The argument upon which Jesus relies for his certainty of a life beyond the grave rests upon the assumption, which was to him beyond question, that God is a living God:[5] and he quotes with entire acquiescence the formula of Deuteronomy, "The Lord our God, the Lord is one".[6]

Looking at this evidence as a whole, may we not say of Jesus' belief about God what we have already found occasion to say in several other connections—first, that, so far as the form of the

---

[1] Mark xv. 34.   [2] x. 18.   [3] x. 27; xiv. 36.
[4] xii. 24.   [5] xii. 26, 27.
[6] xii. 29, quoting Deut. vi. 4.

belief goes, it is cast on conventional lines, and would not have seemed unfamiliar to those among whom Jesus lived and taught; but that, in the second place, the vividness of insight and the force of purpose with which Jesus appropriated the common forms of Jewish religion raised them to a unique value, and made it possible for them to become the natural expression of Christianity? If this be so, it is not only an easier but also a more remarkable conclusion than the alternative one. Almost any sincere man may, by announcing a sufficiently original or extravagant creed, found a new religious sect: it is given to very few so to inspire an old creed with spiritual force and meaning as to regenerate it, and transform it into a new religion.

CHAPTER VIII

JESUS HIMSELF

I

ARE we now in a position to answer the question towards which our whole inquiry has been moving—who was Jesus? Have we sufficiently reviewed all the evidence that is supplied by the second gospel? Are our conclusions, under each head of the subject, homogeneous enough to provide, at any rate, a working hypothesis for a Christology?

Considering Jesus in relation to his home life, his family and his friends, we have seen no reason to doubt the completeness with which he shared the normal interests and ideas of the country people among whom he was brought up.[1] The study of his methods of teaching and habitual mode of life has brought out very strongly

[1] Chap. ii.

JESUS HIMSELF

the reality of his human nature—not only the general setting and form of his activities, which he shared with his fellow-countrymen, but also those special characteristics which marked him out as a man among men.[1] The deeper and much more difficult study of Jesus' mind, that is, of his customary ways of thinking and judging, showed that the outward characteristics were a true index of his intelligence—an intelligence that worked along the ordinary lines of human thought, but with quite extraordinary power and insight.[2] Again, Jesus' social outlook shared the limitations of his age, and he escaped from the necessity of trying to mend the present order of things only by holding with super-prophetic certainty to the vision of a Messianic Kingdom.[3] Further, the key to the understanding of Jesus' moral nature consists in the fact that he was "tempted in all points like as we are," sharing with us the experience of penitence, the attitude of humility, and the weakness of the flesh.[4] And in the inquiry just finished we have set the seal to all that has gone before in concluding that the framework of Jesus' religious beliefs was the dogma and worship of the Jewish synagogue,

[1] Chap. iii.   [2] Chap. iv.   [3] Chap. v.   [4] Chap. vi.

which, however, the power of his faith was able to transfigure into the earliest lineaments of the Catholic Church.[1]

From each of these points of view we have gained the impression of a personality, the greatness of which lies in its power to *grow out of* its limitations, so that men have been led to say not only "this is human," but also "this is divine".

It would seem, then, that we are well on the way towards a final conclusion. But there are three classes of evidence, or perhaps it would be more true to say three ways of reconsidering evidence that has already been examined in part, which must not be overlooked in any impartial view of the whole subject. We have said something, in a particular connection, about Jesus' miracles of healing.[2] We have not yet considered his miracles as a whole, or from an evidential point of view. That is the first of the tasks that remain. The second is to review those passages in which Jesus makes personal claims, and to estimate their importance. The third and hardest of all is to ask, with a view to deciding what we think of Jesus, what he thought of himself—who he supposed himself to be. If some kind

---

[1] Chap. vii. [2] Chap. iii., § 4.

of answer can be given to these questions it may be hoped that we shall at last be in a position to sum up " the conclusion of the whole matter ".

II

It will be convenient to adopt the conventional classification of miracles as miracles of healing and miracles that affect the laws of nature—though we shall do so without supposing that there is any ultimate difference between the two classes. The former class includes medical cases, cases that might be called surgical, or semi-surgical, and a large number of instances of madness or epilepsy. The second class comprises the calming of the sea (if that be properly treated as a miracle), the walking on water, the withering of the fig-tree, the multiplication of food, and the raising of Jairus' daughter.

The number and nature of the miracles of healing will be best seen if they are set out in tabulated form, thus :—

MIRACLES OF HEALING.

No.	Reference.	Subject.	Disease.	Special Conditions.	Method of Cure.	Nature of Cure.	Remarks.
1	i. 23	man	unclean spirit	recognition of Jesus	word (command)	sudden	after convulsions.
2	i. 30	woman	fever		raising by hand	,,	complete cure.
3	i. 40	man	leprosy	man's faith; Jesus' compassion	touch and word	,,	,,
4	ii. 3	,,	paralysis	sequel to forgiveness of sin	word (indirect)	,,	,,
5	iii. 1	,,	withered hand		,,	,,	,,
6	v. 2	,,	unclean spirit	recognition of Jesus	word	gradual (2 stages)	first "command" fails; after parley with evil spirits, compromise is allowed.
7	v. 25	woman	hæmorrhage (chronic)	woman's faith	spontaneous "power"	sudden	complete cure, due to faith; Jesus conscious, but not willing.
8	vii. 25	girl	unclean spirit	"faith" of mother	word (indirect)	gradual?	weakness after cure?
9	vii. 32	man	deafness and stammer	privacy	touching ears and tongue with spittle: prayer (?) and word	sudden	complete cure: a difficult case.
10	viii. 22	,,	blindness	,,	spittle and hands on eyes twice	gradual (2 stages)	complete cure.
11	ix. 17	boy	dumb (and deaf?) spirit	faith of father	(i) word (ii) taking by hand	gradual (2 stages)	by prayer.
12	x. 46	man	blindness	faith of man	word (indirect)	sudden	by faith (as though nothing more needed).

Several interesting points emerge from a consideration of this list.

(i) Only twelve cases are described, and, in the absence of further evidence, we must regard them as typical of the cures which Jesus is said to have been able to work to a practically unlimited extent. The twelve include four cases of some kind of "possession," two of blindness, one of deafness, and five of chronic ailments. Except possibly in the first of these classes— "possession" by evil spirits,—none of the cases could be described as merely nervous disorders ; so that what seems to be claimed on behalf of the worker of these cures (if one is to suppose that the miracles have been reported with any evidential purpose) is something more than the ordinary power of suggestion, or the influence of a stronger over a weaker will. It is also worth noticing, in this connection, that ten out of the twelve patients are adults, and that eight of them are men. Indeed, there is some evidence that the cases have been selected because of their special difficulty : three of them (Nos. 9, 10, 11), are definitely so described ; and in each of these cases Jesus avoids, or tries to avoid, publicity in the working of the cure.

How far the various ailments that are here

described could or could not have been cured by suggestion or will-power, is a purely scientific question, with regard to which it would be more than imprudent to anticipate the decision of medical experience. At present we know little more than our own ignorance on these matters. But it is perhaps safe to say that the present tendency is to find the miracles of healing more, instead of less, credible, when explained along lines of known human agency. And that is, indeed, the sort of way in which these phenomena were interpreted by the much more ignorant people amongst whom they first occurred. The nature of the miracles was more or less familiar, though the ease and certainty with which they were worked were without precedent. Crowds followed Jesus as they had followed no prophet or healer before, because they were sure of his power. But it did not occur to them that because he worked such miracles he must be more than a man. Nor did Jesus himself, according to the second gospel, use his powers as an argument for any such claims. Whilst, then, we recognise that some of the miracles of healing pass beyond the limits ordinarily assigned to the sphere of suggestion and the like, we shall yet expect to be able to explain them all,

JESUS HIMSELF

in the light of a fuller knowledge of human powers, and a fuller appreciation of Jesus' humanity, scientifically.

(ii) We have already had occasion to say something about the part played by faith in the miracles of healing.[1] In half of the cases just enumerated it is stated that some faith was shown, either on the part of the patients (three cases) or on the part of their relations (in the two cases of a boy and a girl, where the parents came to Jesus to ask that they might be healed, and in that of the paralytic, whom his friends let down through the roof into Jesus' presence). But in the other six instances Jesus makes no demand for faith, and it is not said that any was shown. People came to be healed because they knew as a matter of fact that others had been healed. This lower faith, that Jesus probably overlooked, may have won more "miracles" than the higher faith that he commended. In one case, that of the Syro-Phœnician woman (No. 8) the name of faith seems to be given to a spiritual insight which is capable of making a clever retort. Generally speaking, then, S. Mark's account of these selected miracles goes against the idea that they were at all generally performed with a

[1] *Cf.* p. 57.

religious intention—that is, to call out or to inspire faith—and rather bears out our former conclusion that Jesus' works of healing were spontaneous acts of charity, prompted by pity, and bestowed wherever there seemed to be the greatest need.[1]

(iii) It would be interesting, were it possible, to find out upon what principles Jesus applied his methods of healing. The evidence, so far as our twelve cases are concerned, is as follows. Cases of "possession" are always treated by word (Nos. 1, 6, and 11). It may be a direct command to the "evil spirit" to come out of the patient's body: it may be an indirect statement or command by acting upon which the patient is saved. The second part of the cure in No. 11 is the exception that proves this general rule. Jesus' word had been effective in casting out the spirit: his touch was needed to give new strength to the boy.

There is one case (No. 8) in which the cure by word is apparently regarded as effected at a distance. But possibly this is a mistake: Jesus' words show that he knew what was the state of the child, but do not necessarily imply that he affected it. That is to say, it is uncertain

[1] *Cf.* p. 58.

JESUS HIMSELF

whether this incident should be regarded as a work of healing at all.

But though the cure by word was the ordinary method of treatment in cases of possession, it was by the method of touch that Jesus dealt with the great majority of medical cases (Nos. 2, 3, 9, 10, and 11). The touch of the hand, and (in cases of blindness, deafness, or dumbness) the use of spittle, he regarded as the normal sacrament of physical healing. Jesus did not invent these methods. In using them he was in all probability following the customs of other healers among his countrymen. Here, as elsewhere, he took the old forms and applied them with a new power.

There was, then, a clear distinction in Jesus' mind between cases of "possession," and cases of physical disease. In the former instance he felt that he was dealing with an intangible evil spirit, possessing, but not identical with, the body of the patient. This spirit could not be affected by any attempt to cure those physical phenomena which were the signs of its presence. It must be treated personally, and commanded by the good spirit in Jesus to come out of the body in which it dwelt. Afterwards, if the body were weakened or almost dead, it might be strengthened by touch (No. 11). On the other hand, where there was no question of possession, Jesus' power of working physical cures (whatever it may have been) was applied through the sense of touch. There were even cases (of which No. 7 may be taken as a type) where cures were worked spontaneously by the mere contact of Jesus' clothes. Here Jesus was conscious of what had happened: but he had not intended that it should happen. In the case described by S. Mark there was great faith on the part of the patient: but this cannot always have been so:[1] and we must therefore allow that although in many cases Jesus deliberately adopted methods of healing which he felt to be suitable to the particular ailment, yet there were many other cases in which he worked cures consciously (perhaps) but not deliberately, in virtue of a power over which he had less control than the faith of his patients.

(iv) Later writers, who were more anxious to vindicate Jesus' power over evil and disease than to describe the exact methods which he used, preferred to regard all the cures as sudden and complete. As regards the completeness of

[1] Mark iii. 10; vi. 56.

JESUS HIMSELF

the cures, in most cases even the second gospel expresses no doubt about it. But in some instances in which an "evil spirit" has been cast out (and in both the cases which S. Mark mentions, Nos. 8 and 11, the patients are children) the patient remains in a very weak condition, and a second remedy may be needed to complete the cure.

With regard to the suddenness of the cures, there is clear evidence that in particularly difficult cases only gradual remedies were possible. Thus the first attempt to deal with the demoniac of Gadara (No. 6) is a partial failure, and the final form of the cure is represented as a compromise between Jesus and the "evil spirits" who "possess" the man. In two other cases (Nos. 8 and 11) the casting out of a spirit is succeeded by a physical weakness which in one instance, at least, nearly proves fatal. But the clearest case of a gradual cure is that of a blind man (No. 10) which, probably because it lays stress on the incomplete result of the first laying on of Jesus' hands, has been omitted from the narrative in the other Synoptic Gospels.

We conclude that, just as different diseases needed different remedies, so they were capable of a more and of a less sudden cure; that Jesus, who in dealing with physical ailments adopted the methods which he found already in use, did not expect or claim to work cures, as a general rule, except by the stimulation of natural and therefore gradual processes; and that those who best knew the circumstances recognised this, and have preserved a truer account of the miracles of healing than some later writers.

But it should be added that the word "gradual" is here used in a relative sense—distinct, indeed, from "sudden," but also very different from "gradual" in the sense in which a modern physician would use it. We are told of no case in which a *course* of treatment was needed in order to work a cure.

So much may fairly be inferred from the evidence of the second gospel as to the nature of Jesus' miracles of healing. The larger question of their Christological significance must, however, be postponed until we have dealt with the second class of miracles, where the problem arises in a more acute form.

III

Those miracles which, for distinction's sake, we have classed together as "affecting the laws of nature," must be examined from the same point of view as those that we have hitherto

JESUS HIMSELF

been considering. That is to say, we shall try to follow the plain meaning of the narratives given in the second gospel; but where it seems natural to distinguish between those elements of the narratives which belong to the original facts and those which belong to the secondary interpretation of the facts, we shall endeavour to do so. For just as it is undeniable that Jesus cured cases of epilepsy and the like, but disputable whether he was right in treating them, or his biographers right in reporting them, as instances of demonic possession, so we shall not be surprised if some others of the more startling events or moving experiences of the ministry are represented under exaggerated or even mistaken forms of the miraculous.

It is indeed true that in one important sense sound criticism cannot separate the miraculous from the non-miraculous elements in the Gospel. The narrative as a whole is wonderfully coherent. Works are a commentary upon words, and words upon works. There is an absence of self-consciousness, or of straining after effect, in S. Mark's supernaturalism, which carries a conviction of simplicity and primitiveness. And it might be added that it is no more possible to divide one class of miracles from another, within this gospel, than it is to isolate the miraculous elements as a whole. But these characteristics are by no means inconsistent with a certain confusedness between fact and interpretation of fact, and an inability to estimate historical evidence, which commonly mark the chroniclers of traditions.

(i) This difficulty arises in the very first case of the so-called "nature miracles". Certainly once, and perhaps on two occasions in the second gospel, the stormy lake of Galilee is said to have been miraculously calmed. In both instances the narrative bears all the marks of originality and first-hand evidence, and must be founded upon a real experience.[1] Moreover, the treatment of inanimate objects as if they were animate which is involved in Jesus' rebuke to the wind and sea is quite in accordance with his practice elsewhere—as for instance with regard to the fig-tree,[2] or (indirectly) the mountain.[3] Indeed, the very word that is here addressed to the sea had already been spoken (in a less

---

[1] Mark iv. 35-39; vi. 45-52. Notice that Jesus, in accordance with the context, is already in the boat; and that he is asleep on the "cushion"—details difficult of invention.

[2] xi. 14.   [3] xi. 23.

emphatic sense) to a man possessed by an unclean spirit.[1]

But if one tries to go behind the traditional account of what happened, it appears that in the second of the two incidents the language does not necessarily imply a miracle at all. The sudden falling of the wind (itself a likely enough phenomenon) at the time when Jesus was taken into the ship may have been no more than a coincidence.[2] And thus one is disposed to think that a similar explanation may apply to the earlier incident also. Only, there is this difference in the earlier case: not only S. Mark's authority (we may suppose, S. Peter) regarded it as miraculous; but also, unless the evidence is quite untrustworthy, Jesus himself took the same view. This is a possibility that has to be faced. There may have been experiences in Jesus' life which he took to be supernatural, but which, from our own point of view, allow of a natural explanation.

It would be unfair to ignore the further possibility that these incidents may have been interpreted either by those who witnessed them or by those who edited the traditional accounts, in the light of certain passages in the Old Testament. " Thou rulest the pride of the sea : when

---

[1] Mark i. 25. [2] But *cf.* p. 215.

the waves thereof arise, thou stillest them"[1] is part of the ground of (David) the Servant's trust in the Lord. The knowledge of such a passage might incline Jesus or his disciples to accept a natural coincidence as a supernatural occurrence. And the story of Jonah—which was in other respects, according to S. Matthew, taken as having prophetical application to Jesus[2]—includes a rather close parallel to the first of the incidents under discussion. "The Lord sent out a great wind into the sea, and there was a mighty tempest in the sea, so that the ship was like to be broken. . . . But Jonah was gone down into the innermost parts of the ship; and he lay, and was fast asleep. So the shipmaster came to him, and said unto him, What meanest thou, O sleeper? arise, call upon thy God, if so be that God will think upon us, that we perish not."[3] It is, of course, obvious that the outcome of the story, and the manner of its treatment, is quite unlike that in the Gospel: but the similarity of language is sufficient to make it possible that there is some connection between them. Of what kind or importance such a connection may be will depend partly upon whether similar connections can be traced in the case of other miraculous events in the Gospel.

[1] Ps. lxxxix. 9.   [2] Matt. xii. 39, 40; xvi. 4.   [3] Jonah i. 4-6.

JESUS HIMSELF

(ii) Closely connected with the last two incidents in some respects is the story of Jesus walking on the sea.[1] This narrative, again, bears every mark of being founded on a genuine reminiscence. That Jesus did appear to the disciples to be walking on the sea, it is difficult not to believe: but one may very well suppose that their experience has been misinterpreted and confused in later tradition.

Thus it is significant that S. Luke, who took great pains to arrive at a true knowledge of the facts related in the gospels, and who was specially acquainted with matters of navigation in general, and with this lake in particular[2], reproduces the previous story of the stilling of the storm, and follows S. Mark up to the end of the feeding of the 5,000 which immediately precedes the present incident, but at this point becomes silent.[3] True, this silence covers a large body of tradition against which no such difficulty can be urged (from Mark vi. 45, to viii. 10 inclusive): but it is at least noteworthy that it should begin at this point.

---

[1] Mark vi. 45-50. [2] *Cf.* his technical corrections of S. Mark in viii. 22-25, and his accounts of S. Paul's sea journeys in Acts. [3] Luke ix.

Few narratives in the gospels have given rise to such a variety of naturalistic interpretations as this: but it cannot be said that any of them are convincing. Yet probably the true explanation lies not very far below the surface. For the most important feature of the narrative is the internal evidence which it affords for a possible explanation. The essential fact of the story—the appearance of Jesus to his friends on the lake at night—admits quite naturally of a telepathic interpretation. The dangerous position of the disciples; their remembrance, in this moment of great anxiety, of the previous occasion when Jesus had been with them, and had stilled the storm; the desire to have him with them again, on the one hand; on the other, Jesus giving himself to solitary prayer, watching the boat on its stormy passage across the lake, and seeing the danger of his friends;[1]— these conditions, as a whole, were just such as to give rise to psychical phenomena. The walking on the *surface* of a stormy sea,[2] which is part of the narrative, and would be necessary

---

[1] Jesus being in the "mountain," this would be possible for some considerable part of the voyage, even at night-time.

[2] This is the proper meaning of "walking *on* (ἐπί) the sea".

in the case of a material body, is impossible to picture: in the case of a "phantasm" there is no real difficulty in imagining the scene. The curious fact, which S. Mark alone records, that the phantasm "would have passed by them," perhaps points to the existence of an older and truer tradition in which there was no receiving of Jesus, in material form, into the ship. "They supposed that it was an apparition," says the present story. Probably in the original version it really was such. But experience and interpretation seem to have become so confused that no reconstruction can be more than conjectural.

(iii) The story of the withering of the fig-tree is one of the most perplexing in the Gospel.[1] That it is based on a real incident can hardly be doubted; but there are several indications that this incident may have been misinterpreted. Thus, in the original version of the story, Jesus' words to the fig-tree (which, as we noticed before, is treated animistically) are not, strictly speaking, a command, or a curse (as Peter thought),[2] but the expression of a wish. There is nothing foretold about the accomplishment of the wish,

---

[1] Mark xi. 12-14, 20-25. [2] xi. 21.

whether by the withering of the tree, or in any other way. There is nothing to show that Jesus intended such a result. Again, Jesus' words are spoken privately, and to the tree : they are overheard (it is implied, accidentally) by the disciples.[1] Thus, though Peter claims the withering of the tree as the result of Jesus' words, and Jesus apparently accepts this explanation, yet the connection between the two things as cause and effect is not actually stated. This may make room for possible alternative explanations. If it is possible that a cold night, or some other natural cause, killed the premature leaves of the tree, the growth of the supernatural explanation of the story is easily accounted for. Indeed, we can see a further embellishment of the story in the first gospel, which represents the tree, at the moment when Jesus' words (now changed to a definite command) are spoken, as immediately withering away.[2]

There remains a difficulty that has already occurred in another connection.[3] The event is (let us assume) a natural event ; but Jesus at any rate accepts it as a miraculous fulfilment of his wish. That Jesus himself may have misunderstood some of his own experiences, and

[1] Mark xi. 14.   [2] Matt. xxi. 19.   [3] *v*. p. 213.

regarded more phenomena as due to the direct action of God than persons of smaller faith would be disposed to do, is not a very hard hypothesis. But there is perhaps an alternative. There seems to be no certain connection between the incident of the fig-tree and the teaching about faith which accompanies it in the second gospel,[1] Sayings about faith are almost " commonplaces," and occur in other contexts in the first and third gospels;[2] nor is it easy to suppose that the present loosely connected passage gives an adequate account of the incident and the teaching based upon it. Evidently S. Luke was puzzled by the narrative. In his account the actual incident is omitted: but the fig-tree reappears in a compiled saying as " this sycamore tree," and it (not a mountain) is to be " rooted up " . . . and planted " in the sea ".[3] Yet " this " mountain, and " this " sycamore tree, forms of speech which persist in all versions of the saying, seem to point to the place of its origin in the second gospel—the slopes of the Mount of Olives, and the solitary fig-tree. So that one is inclined to think either that the true motive and meaning of the incident have been lost, or that a natural

---

[1] Mark xi. 23. [2] Matt. xvii. 20; Luke xvii. 5.
[3] Luke xvii. 6.

220 JESUS ACCORDING TO S. MARK

event was taken by Jesus and the disciples as supernatural. In any case the thing remains incongruous and perplexing.

(iv) The two miracles of feeding—that of the 5,000 and that of the 4,000—may be taken together. In spite of some differences in detail there seems to be no sufficient reason to doubt that both narratives are based on one and the same incident. It is at least possible that S. Luke held this opinion, since he entirely omits the narrative of the 4,000. But even if it were not so, yet the two stories involve the same issues, and may most profitably be discussed together.[1]

We have to notice, first, that there is no miracle for which we ought to have better evidence than the first of these. It is recorded by all four evangelists in considerable detail: it was, *ex hypothesi*, worked in public, before 5,000 people, many of whom (at least) must have realised the miracle, and have borne witness to it in after years. Besides, the thing was so manifestly supernatural that there could be no room for a mistake. If the 5,000 were fed at all, they must have been fed miraculously. Either, then, the occurrence fell out as described, or the whole story must be rejected as unhistorical. This is a plainer issue than has

[1] Mark vi. 35 = Matt. xiv. 15 = Luke ix. 12.

hitherto been reached in dealing with these miracles. What considerations can be urged towards arriving at a solution?

In the first place, the incident of the 5,000 as it stands bears some evidence of displacement. There is really no sufficient motive for the miracle as described by S. Mark, who places it on the evening of the same day as the voyage across the lake. Of the 4,000 it is said that they had been three days in the desert, and that some of their homes were far away:[1] the 5,000 had not come farther than half a day's journey from their homes, and had not spent more than a few hours in the desert. Nor is it likely that on the first evening of their retirement across the lake, after a time of crowded ministry and enforced fasting,[2] the disciples would be found so ill supplied with provisions that they have only five loaves and two fishes, and that the twelve baskets which they carry with them are empty, until filled with the remnants of the miraculous feast.[3] The presence of the empty baskets suggests that the incident belongs to the end, not the beginning, of a period of retirement.

[1] Mark viii. 2, 3. It is, of course, possible that some elements belonging to the account of the 5,000 have been transferred to that of the 4,000, or *vice versa*.
[2] vi. 31.   [3] vi. 43 (*pace* viii. 14.)

Again, one cannot ignore some elements of artificiality that seem to be present in the story. To feed 5,000 people five loaves are required; in one narrative there are twelve baskets—one for each of the twelve disciples; in the other there are seven baskets—one for the fragments of each of the seven loaves. And some numerical significance—in connection, apparently, with the multiplication of the food—underlies the arrangement of the people " in ranks, by hundreds and by fifties ". (For no reason is given why the crowd should be counted.)[1]

Lastly, there is a parallel to this miracle of feeding in the story of Elisha, which cannot be ignored, though different opinions may be held as to the degree in which it is likely to have affected the form, if not the substance, of the present narrative. " There came a man," says the chronicler, " from Baal-shalishah, and brought the man of God bread of the firstfruits, twenty loaves of barley, and fresh ears of corn in his sack. And he said, Give unto the people, that they may eat. And his ser-

---

[1] An alternative reason for this might be found in 1 Kings xviii. 4—" Obadiah took an hundred prophets, and hid them by fifty in a cave, and fed them with bread and water."

vant said, What, should I set this before an hundred men? But he said, Give the people, that they may eat; for thus saith the Lord, They shall eat, and shall leave thereof. So he set it before them, and they did eat, and left thereof, according to the word of the Lord."[1]

To allow that the second gospel might contain an imitative legend (even though it be based on some real event) is to admit an element of uncertainty into our interpretation of it, such as we have not contemplated hitherto. But it is a possibility, and it cannot be ignored.

(v) There remains only the account of the raising of Jairus' daughter.[2] This miracle, like the last, is fully attested. But the alterations introduced by S. Matthew and S. Luke do not add anything of importance to the original narrative, and do not seem to be based on any new evidence. We are really dealing with a single tradition variously edited.

According to this tradition, there was no doubt in the minds of any of those present that the girl was really dead. Jesus' suggestion, "the child is not dead, but sleepeth," is laughed to scorn. S. Luke himself, in all probability a physician, adds that they knew that she was

[1] 2 Kings iv. 42-44. [2] Mark v. 35.

dead,[1] and does not suggest the possibility of a mistake.

It would be attractive to take Jesus' words literally, and to suppose that when he came into the room [2] he saw that the girl was not really dead, but only in some kind of trance. But it is more likely that Jesus was using the words in a spiritual rather than a literal sense, and that to him all death seemed to be, in some sense, a state of sleep, from which the divine power might rouse those who seemed to be beyond recall. It does not follow, of course, that the girl really was dead. The hypothesis of a fit or trance might still be adopted. Only we should have to hold that Jesus, believing as an act of faith that this " death " was only " sleep," and acting upon that belief, did not as a matter of fact raise a dead person, but revived one who was in a trance. The miracle would then fall under the commoner class of works of healing, and might admit of an explanation on lines already indicated.

Is it possible, from this examination of the miracles in the second gospel, to draw any safe

---

[1] Luke viii. 53. But it is easy to exaggerate S. Luke's " medical knowledge," which was not incompatible with a very credulous attitude towards miracles.

[2] This is probably the right order of events, Mark v. 39.

JESUS HIMSELF

conclusions as to the kind of powers which Jesus manifested, and therefore as to the kind of person that Jesus was? At one end of the scale we have certain works of healing, about the literal truth of which no doubt seems to be possible. At the other end we meet with a few detached stories (for it will hardly be suggested that these, like those of the miracles of healing, are casual instances representative of many more) which claim for Jesus powers for which there is no precedent. It would, of course, be unscientific, upon our present hypothesis, to reject these latter stories simply because they are more difficult to believe. We must try to judge them from the point of view gained by our previous inquiry as a whole. And more particularly, we must consider how far the " miracles affecting the laws of nature " can be explained as a mere extension of principles already recognised in the " miracles of healing ".

As to the first point, it would be a fair summary of our previous conclusions [1] to say that the second gospel represents Jesus as one whose life was, to all outward appearance, an entirely human one, and whose divine claim rested not upon any original freedom from the limitations of

[1] *Cf.* p. 200.

that life, but upon the spiritual intensity of living by which that life was transformed. This conclusion—whatever be its exact expression—gives a standard of judgment in dealing with such a question as the present. We shall expect to find Jesus working "miracles" which are extensions, on the same plane of experience, and under the same general conditions, of ascertained human achievements. We shall not expect him to act in a way which is out of proportion to his way of teaching, his way of thinking, and his way of life. We cannot imagine any part of his activities to have been out of scale, incongruous, "unlike himself". But that is just what some of the alleged miracles seem to be, in the form in which they have been reported to us. It may be possible in some instances to trace a congruous substratum beneath the incongruous upper layers of tradition. The stilling of the storm may be a misunderstanding : the story of the walking on the sea may be based on a genuine psychical experience : the raising of Jairus' daughter may be an exaggeration of a miracle of healing. But in such cases as the withering of the fig-tree and the feeding of the 5,000 it seems necessary either to attribute to Jesus powers which there is no other reason to suppose that he possessed—which in-

JESUS HIMSELF

deed are entirely unlike and underivable from others which it is certain that he possessed—or to regard the narrative as untrustworthy in these particulars. The latter is by far the easier alternative. It is perfectly legitimate to hold that the early tradition, as represented by the second gospel, bears witness to the proper limits of Jesus' powers, and sets a standard by which all "miraculous" stories can be judged; and at the same time to admit that, judged by that very standard, a few of the miracles as described even in the early tradition must be pronounced to be unhistorical.

The standard that we wish to set up will, of course, need corroboration from other branches of evidence which we cannot consider here. Thus it is obvious that some light is thrown on the miracles in the second gospel by what is said about Jesus' ministry in S. Peter's speeches in the Acts—especially when one remembers the traditional connection between S. Peter and S. Mark. And one can argue back from the kind of "signs" that accompanied the early preaching of Christianity to their probable form before the Resurrection. It must in any case be insisted that the distinction between the canonical and the uncanonical books of the New Testament is not such that all miracles recorded in the former are necessarily more credible than all recorded in the latter. There must be an independent standard of judgment, and that must be derived from one's understanding of Jesus' personality as a whole.

The position that seems generally to be taken up by critics of the miracles is first, One would like to believe these things, on religious grounds; and secondly, But one cannot, on scientific grounds. Whereas the truer position would seem to be, first, One would rather not believe such things, on religious grounds; and secondly, One can explain what is true in them, on scientific grounds.

To put it plainly, some of the supposed miracles *are not worthy of Jesus.* They are not part of man's best ideas about God, but of his less educated imaginings. They are the measure of his misunderstanding of those spiritual miracles which are the proper proof of a spiritual revelation. God does not show himself to be Incarnate by working on a different plane from man. He is most truly revealed when he is most truly man.

IV

It might be thought that the whole question which we are discussing is capable of an easy solution. The claims that Jesus made for himself, the devotion which he directed towards himself, might be held to determine the nature of his own personality. But what, so far as the second gospel is concerned, are the real facts? Jesus nowhere formulates his claims, never explains himself in the most rudimentary terms of a creed, never draws up any rules of membership or prospectus of the "Kingdom of God," and refuses (except by implication) to state his authority for overriding the customs of the Established Church.[1]

There is, however, some evidence to show in what relation Jesus held himself to stand to his mission, and what proportion of personal devotion to himself he allowed or encouraged. But it is informal and indirect, resting on "general impressions" and implicit claims.

(i) In the first place, Jesus is always the central figure in the gospel. And he is such not because the writer of the gospel deliberately made him so (there is no sign of literary craftsmanship on the part of S. Mark), but because he

[1] Mark xi. 27-33.

was so in real life. Further, the impression that one gets from the second gospel is that he was so consciously, not unconsciously. There is perhaps a change of attitude in this respect as between the earlier and later parts of the gospel. Up to the time of the Transfiguration Jesus generally represents himself as a prophet, a teacher, a healer; he is the servant of men, the unwilling object of their enthusiasm. Afterwards he becomes more and more the Messiah, the Master; his teaching is more personal, the references to his coming Passion more frequent. And, in proportion to this development, discipleship comes to be regarded as a personal attitude of belief in Jesus, rather than an abstract moral fitness for the Kingdom of God.

This new teaching might be said to begin with the question, "Whom do men say that I am?"[1] It matters, Jesus implies, whether or not men have a right idea of his personal claims. It is necessary for a disciple to understand that his Messiahship is different from the ordinary conceptions of what it should be.[2] The Transfiguration, whatever its exact significance, at any rate implies a personal glorification of Jesus, and is so interpreted by the disciples; for they are

[1] Mark viii. 27.   [2] viii. 31.

moved to an act of homage towards him quite undreamt of hitherto.¹ From this time onwards Jesus' mind is full of his coming Passion and death. Nor are these personal forebodings put away, or subordinated, as being of selfish interest ; but they are emphasised again and again,² and regarded as essential, and made the basis of the instruction of the disciples. Gradually the idea of the Kingdom as a spiritual but very real institution, whose inauguration is close at hand,³ leads up to Jesus' entry into Jerusalem, when he seems to court the public recognition that he had avoided hitherto.⁴ From this time date the personal parables,⁵ the personal interpretations of Scripture,⁶ and the prophetic claim (illustrated by the apocalyptic discourse)—" my words shall not pass away ".⁷ It is at this time that Jesus accepts the personal homage of the woman who anoints his head,⁸ that he claims special acts of service and hospitality,⁹ that he pronounces a woe upon the man who betrays him,¹⁰

---

¹ Mark ix. 5. The intention of "building a tabernacle" for Jesus seems to be in order that they may secure his continued presence, as a divine spirit.

² viii. 31, 38 ; ix. 9, 31 ; x. 33, 39, etc.
³ *Cf.* the incident in x. 35-40.   ⁴ xi. 7-10.
⁵ xii. 1-9.   ⁶ xii. 10, 11, 35-37.   ⁷ xiii. 31.   ⁸ xiv. 3-9.
⁹ xi. 3 ; xiv. 14.   ¹⁰ xiv. 21.

and that he institutes the personal commemoration of the sacrifice of his body and blood.[1]

Jesus, then, within the limits of his lifelong sacrifice and humility, was not self-forgetful, self-depreciating, or indecisive: rather he was self-assertive, self-conscious, confident. In teaching he was noticeably dogmatic—but only in the laying down of principles which demanded individual application. In action he was easy, simple, decisive. In his manner and way of life he was always ready, never at a loss, entirely "master of the situation". One gets from the gospel a very strong impression that he was "a born leader," and that he knew it.

(ii) Secondly, discipleship, more particularly in the later part of the gospel, means personal devotion to Jesus. From the very beginning of the ministry the "call" of the disciples is a call to personal allegiance. "Come ye after me," says Jesus to Simon and Andrew,[2] "Follow me" to Levi the son of Alphæus.[3] He compares the relation of the disciples to himself with that of the "sons of the bridechamber" to the bridegroom.[4] He is the central figure: their duty is to help and minister to him. The apostolic life, to which the twelve are definitely

[1] Mark xiv. 22-24.   [2] i. 17.   [3] ii. 14.   [4] ii. 19.

appointed, is to "be with him" quite as much as to go "forth to preach":[1] they are to learn by living with him. Of discipleship in general both the motive and the manner are stated in personal terms—" If any man would come after me, let him deny himself, and take up his cross, and follow me ".[2] The familiarity of this demand makes us overlook its real meaning. Discipleship means the limitation or even the surrender of a man's personal independence in order that he may become a follower of Jesus. It is not a demand for friendship or for allegiance, but for service : Jesus always leads—even in the bearing of the cross—the disciple always follows. Again, stress is laid upon personal loyalty to Jesus,— " Whosoever shall be ashamed of me and of my words . . . the Son of man also shall be ashamed of him. . . ."[3] It is suggested as an encouragement and sanction of charitable acts that they become acts of kindness to Jesus himself, and through him to God.[4] It is assumed that others besides disciples will experience the power that comes through formal allegiance to Jesus, and will thus be led to a deeper loyalty.[5] It is good for little children that they should come to Jesus

[1] Mark iii. 14. [2] viii. 34. [3] viii. 38.
[4] ix. 37. [5] ix. 39.

and be blessed by him,[1] and good for men that they should surrender all that is valuable in this life for his sake and the Gospel's.[2] In answering the request of James and John, who ask that their earthly precedence may be continued in the Kingdom (for they, with Peter, formed the inner group of the disciples), Jesus lays special stress on the imitation and sharing of his own sufferings that is entailed by discipleship.[3]

Indeed, it is an invariable mark of Jesus' teaching that he attributes no value to self-sacrifice or goodness for their own sake, but simply because they bring men to follow him, and make them fit to enter into the Kingdom of God. The disciples have nothing to gain, apart from himself. The Kingdom has no certainty, except through his suffering and death. Everything in the last resort turns upon his own personality.

This, then, is the crucial question upon which the whole meaning of the Gospel depends. How did Jesus think about himself? Who did he know himself to be?

V

In dealing with Jesus' knowledge of himself we are not dealing with a fixed state of mind,

---

[1] Mark x. 14. [2] x. 29. [3] x. 38.

JESUS HIMSELF

but with one which grew. This point seems to be established by the following considerations.

First, from the evidence as to Jesus' early life which we have already considered,[1] it appears that neither Jesus' relations nor his fellow-townsmen knew of anything superhuman in him, or in the circumstances of his thirty years' life at Nazareth. It does not, of course, necessarily follow that Jesus' idea of himself was what others supposed it to be: but it is difficult to think otherwise. All probability is in favour of the view that Jesus only came to understand himself gradually, as he "advanced in wisdom and stature, and in favour with God and men".[2]

Secondly, the outcome of our whole inquiry has been a conviction as to the reality and fulness of Jesus' humanity. In mind, in morals, in social and religious outlook, the main fact is that he shares to the full the experience of his class and nationality. There is therefore a strong presumption in favour of the normal growth of his self-consciousness. It is unreasonable, if not impossible, to posit a mind that is partly fixed and partly subject to growth.

Thirdly, a careful examination of the way in which Jesus speaks of himself shows, even within

[1] *Cf.* Chap. ii.   [2] Luke ii. 52.

the short limits of the recorded ministry, quite definite stages of growth. The Baptism, the Transfiguration, and the entry into Jerusalem mark the forward steps in this development. The use of the title "Son of man" almost exclusively in the latter part of the ministry, and in connection with the impending Passion and death, is only one illustration of it. It will be our business to examine the evidence under this head in detail. We will only remark here how great a growth of self-consciousness would be shown by the history of the thirty years, if we could investigate them as carefully as we can the thirty months that compose the historic ministry.

We are dealing, then, with a mind that grew. And we are trying to gauge its full meaning from a fragmentary account of a small part of its development, much as one conjectures the dip of unseen strata from the scanty evidence of a quarried hillside.

VI

It can hardly be doubted that S. Mark regards the Baptism of Jesus as the first great turning-point in his self-knowledge.[1] The narrative

[1] Mark i. 9-11.

begins at this point, not because, as in the fourth gospel, it was then that the early disciples first met Jesus,[1] but because it really began there in the experience of Jesus himself. It must be remembered that the only possible authority for the vision of heaven opened at the Baptism, and for the Temptation which immediately followed it, was, according to S. Mark's account, Jesus himself. If Jesus spoke about these incidents to his friends, but remained silent as to the thirty years that preceded them, it was almost certainly because the baptism of John was, in Jesus' own experience, the starting-point of his new life, and of his conscious acceptance of the divine sonship. The thirty years had no doubt been a time of preparation, and that none the less valuable for being unenlightened by any full consciousness of Messiahship. The preaching of the kingdom, and the baptism for remission of sins by which John tried to inaugurate it, brought all the previous years' growth to a climax. In the blaze of enthusiasm that was kindled the preceding and preparatory stages may even have seemed dark and unimportant. At any rate, nothing was said about them. The life of Jesus, so far as it was generally known to the world,

[1] John i. 35-42.

began with the baptism of repentance and ended with the cry of despair on the Cross.

The words of Isaiah which Jesus appropriates to himself at his Baptism seem clearly to convey the idea of his Messiahship. We must suppose, then, that this was in some sense the state of his self-knowledge from the beginning of the ministry. But it also seems probable that he did not yet hold this new idea about himself very firmly or fully. It was only by degrees that he came to realise its meaning. The Temptation itself was an early study in the possibilities of the Messiahship—its susceptibility to temptation, and its power to conquer sin. And during the first part of the ministry Jesus is still experimenting, verifying, mastering his own powers and personality.

i. 24. A man with an unclean spirit in the synagogue at Capernaum cries out, recognising Jesus, and calling him, "Jesus of Nazareth (his earthly title) . . . the Holy one of God" (his Messianic claim). Jesus commands the man to be silent, wishing (it appears) to avoid publicity, and disliking such recognition by an unholy spirit. It is implied that he knows the recognition to be right, but that he does not wish to claim it. This is further borne out by—

i. 34, which says of a number of similar incidents that "he suffered not the devils to speak, because they knew him" (some good MSS. add, "to be Christ"). Two other instances occur in the same part of the ministry—

iii. 11. "The unclean spirits, whensoever they beheld him, fell down before him, and cried, saying, Thou art the Son of God. And he charged them much that they should not make him known." This, again, is a Messianic title, which Jesus accepts, but which he does not use of himself.

v. 7. The Gerasene demoniac: "When he saw Jesus from afar, he ran and worshipped him; and crying out with a loud voice, he saith, What have I to do with thee, Jesus, thou Son of the Most High God?" In this case Jesus does not command silence, but parleys with the spirit, probably because he is no longer in Galilee, and there is no fear of popular enthusiasm.

Thus it appears from these instances that during the first period of his ministry Jesus was constantly confronted with the idea of his Messiahship; that he made no attempt to deny the title; but that he took every precaution to prevent its being publicly claimed for him. This is quite consistent with his being conscious of his Messiahship, but being still uncertain as to its exact meaning and use.

Is any further light thrown on this position by other passages from the same part of the gospel?

i. 38. After a busy evening's work in Capernaum, Jesus leaves the town very early the next morning, and departs into a desert place to pray. The disciples follow and find him, and he says, " Let us go elsewhere into the next towns, that I may preach there also ; for to this end came I forth ". Here the last word ($\dot{\epsilon}\xi\hat{\eta}\lambda\theta o\nu$) is sometimes taken in a sense which it might bear in the fourth gospel,[1] but hardly here, as meaning Jesus' coming into the world : either of two alternative interpretations is preferable—that the word refers to Jesus' mission and ministry in general, or (less probably) that it means simply his coming out of Capernaum a few hours before.

ii. 10. The healing of a paralytic man becomes a proof of the claim that "the Son of man hath power on earth to forgive sins". "Power" means here authority ; and this is regarded as delegated " on earth " to " the Son of man," whilst God still binds or looses in heaven. The

---

[1] *E.g.*, John viii. 42 ; xiii. 3.

JESUS HIMSELF

title "Son of man" is used argumentatively, as though to point the contrast between man and God. Jesus regards himself as "the typical man": in claiming the power of forgiveness under that title he is not claiming something for himself as distinct from men, but for himself as man, and for all men through him. "Son of man" was his favourite title in speaking of himself (on the rare occasions when he did so in this detached way, in the third person); and the thought which it contains represents his most permanent knowledge of his own personality.

ii. 17. "I came not to call the righteous, but sinners." Compare a later saying—"The Son of man came not to be ministered unto, but to minister".[1] In both cases the word used bears essentially the same meaning as the "came I forth" already mentioned:[2] and since in the second case the reference is clearly to Jesus' mission and ministry, it is probably so in all three cases. Jesus certainly knew that he had been "sent," and that he had "come" or "come forth" to do a special work for God. He may even have spoken of himself as "coming out" of his thirty years' retirement into the new life of the ministry. But we must beware of attaching to

[1] Mark x. 45.   [2] i. 38, above.

these words the alien idea of a coming from one world or state of existence into another.

ii. 19. Jesus pictures himself as a bridegroom, and the disciples — his special friends—as the "sons of the bride-chamber". He is with them for a time, and they have a right to enjoy his company. But the time is coming when he will "be taken away from them". The imagery is taken from a passage in the Old Testament, in which God seems to be represented as the bridegroom, and the Jewish "remnant" as the bride, in the Messianic kingdom.[1] In using it, Jesus is probably conscious of its Messianic meaning. He is also conscious, we must suppose, of his coming death. If so, this is the earliest evidence that we have of such knowledge, which is not explicitly made known until the second period of the ministry.

ii. 25. The ground of Jesus' appeal to the case of David, to justify his high-handed treatment of the Sabbath, is probably not any analogy between himself and David, David's followers and his own disciples. It is better explained by the use of the title "Son of man" in the saying with which the incident ends. The proper force of this is only brought out in the

---

[1] Hosea ii. 19.

JESUS HIMSELF

second gospel.¹ The title is used, as in a previous connection,² argumentatively. It is not in being more than man, but in being typical man, that Jesus is "lord even of the Sabbath". If any further claim were to have been made here, it could have been made very forcibly by the use of the title "Son of David". But no such idea was in Jesus' mind. He is merely claiming man's right to use—not to be the slave of—his own instruments.

iii. 28. Taken in connection with the previous incident, this passage implies that Jesus attributes his miracles to the working of the "Holy Spirit" in him, and that he regards it as blasphemous to attribute them to the powers of evil. If S. Matthew and S. Luke are right in the saying which they agree in adding at this place, Jesus further distinguishes misrepresentation of himself (under the title of the "Son of man") from misrepresentation of the "Holy Spirit" which works through him.³ But it may be no more than a

---

¹ Mark ii. 28 = Matt. xii. 8 = Luke vi. 5. Matthew and Luke spoil the argumentative use of the title by cutting it off from the preceding words, and by omitting Mark's "*even* of the Sabbath".

² ii. 10, above.

³ Compare what is said of the Holy Spirit at the time of the Baptism, Mark i. 10, 12.

variant of the earlier saying, due to a misunderstanding of the phrase "the sons of men".[1]

vi. 1. The incident of Jesus' visit to Nazareth has already furnished evidence as to how Jesus was regarded by his relations and fellow-townsmen. It is not uninstructive as regards Jesus' idea of his own personality. In the first place, he admits the human relationship which makes it so difficult for the people of Nazareth to credit his new powers. Nazareth is his "own country," Mary, James, Joses, Judas, Simon, and the "sisters" are "his own kin" (the word means relationship by birth), the house in which his sisters still live is "his own house".[2] Whatever else he may have thought about himself, he started at any rate from this common experience, and knew himself to be what his fellow-townsmen said that he was. Secondly, "he marvelled because of their unbelief". Why should he have been surprised, when he admitted what seems to have been the ground of their unbelief—his previous life at Nazareth? Clearly he himself thought this no bar to belief. His present claims, he held, were not inconsistent with his past life, but sprang directly out of it. He was not conscious of any

[1] Mark iii. 28.   [2] vi. 4.

inconsistency between the old life and the new. And thirdly, the title under which he chose to sum up his present claims was that of "Prophet". This probably capitulates, better than any other word, Jesus' self-knowledge during the early part of the ministry. He knew himself to have a special mission from God: he heard himself addressed, and came to think of himself, in the Messianic terms of the Jewish Scriptures: but as yet he does not seem to have understood to the full, or have been ready to teach to others, the meaning of his Messiahship. He prefers to speak of himself formally, when he does so at all, as the "Son of man," and his work is best described as that of a "Prophet".

We have now to see how far our hypothesis of the gradual growth of the Messianic consciousness is borne out by the evidence to be derived from the second part of the gospel.

VII

viii. 27. It is on the journey to Cæsarea Philippi that Jesus for the first time shows an interest in what people are saying about himself. He questions the disciples first as to the state of public opinion, and then as to their personal belief. As to public opinion, there are three theories—either that he is John the Baptist, or that he is Elijah, or that he is "one of the prophets". The last suggestion seems to come rather near to Jesus' own words spoken on the visit to Nazareth :[1] yet he implicitly rejects them all as untrue in his question to Peter : " But who say ye that I am ? " Peter's answer, then, must be accepted as the true one—" Thou art the Christ ". The apostles have come to agree with the opinion of the evil spirits.[2] And, like the latter, they are forbidden to make their knowledge public. It is dangerous knowledge. Its publication must lead to the dilemma—political revolution, or death. (It did in fact lead to the latter.) This passage, then, falls into line with others in which Jesus is conscious of his Messiahship, but does not wish to make it known. The new feature consists in his being willing to share his knowledge with the disciples.

viii. 31. There follows immediately upon this the first of those passages in which Jesus speaks of his coming Passion. There are five

---

[1] Mark vi. 1, above.
[2] i. 24 and other passages, above.

such passages in all,[1] showing how vivid and constant at this time was the idea of Jesus' future sufferings. And it is noticeable that in all of them he speaks of himself as the "Son of man," as though to show that it is as man that he will suffer and die—to win some new right for man, as he had under the same title vindicated man's right to forgive sins, and to determine his own treatment of the Sabbath.[2] The exact relation of these passages to one another is best shown if they are set out side by side.[3] It will be seen that the first and the last are the most detailed. The last indeed, develops so close a correspondence to the actual scenes of the Passion as to suggest that it has been elaborated from a later knowledge of the events. (Notice particularly the mention of the part played by the Romans, which is quite absent from the other predictions.)

viii. 38. As the prediction of Jesus' Passion, so also the prophecy of his Parousia follows closely on the discovery of his Messiahship by the disciples. It too is connected with the title the "Son of man". "Whosoever shall be ashamed of me and of my words in this adul-

---

[1] Mark ix. 9, 12, 31; x. 33; besides the present passage.
[2] ii. 10, 25, above. [3] *Vide* next page.

viii. 31.	ix. 9.	ix. 12.
The Son of man must suffer many things, and be rejected by the elders, and the chief priests, and the scribes, and be killed, and after three days rise again	the Son of man should have risen again from the dead	the Son of man that he should suffer many things and be set at naught

terous and sinful generation, the Son of man also shall be ashamed of him, when he cometh in the glory of his Father with the holy angels." It would be difficult to attach any argumentative meaning to the use of the title in this passage. Probably, since the title has been used in speaking of the Passion, it is used of the Parousia also, to show the essential connection that exists between the two events as stages in the achievement of the Kingdom of God. But the interest

JESUS HIMSELF

ix. 31.	x. 33.
The Son of man is delivered up into the hands of men,	the Son of man shall be delivered unto the chief priests and the scribes; and they shall condemn him to death, and shall deliver him unto the Gentiles: and they shall mock him, and shall spit upon him, and shall scourge him,
and they shall kill him; and when he is killed, after three days he shall rise again	and shall kill him; and after three days he shall rise again

of the passage lies rather in the fact that the Son of man is here spoken of for the first time in relation to his Father. The nearest parallel to this is the statement that of the day and hour of the Parousia " knoweth no one, not even the angels in heaven, neither the Son, but the Father ".[1] There are only two other passages in the second gospel which speak of the Father. To the disciples he is once described as " your

[1] Mark xiii. 32.

Father which is in heaven "; [1] and in the prayer of Gethsemane Jesus addresses him as "Abba, Father".[2] This poverty of use is the more remarkable when we consider that in S. Matthew God is spoken of as Father forty-five times, in S. Luke seventeen times, and in S. John no less than 118 times. S. Mark, then, uses the title seldom. But he uses it significantly. It can hardly be a coincidence that Jesus is represented as calling God "the Father" just in those connections in which he calls himself "the Son of man"—his Passion and his Parousia. They are the essential experiences of his Messiahship, and it is fair to conclude that he was conscious of the fatherhood of God chiefly in those connections. The meaning of the title, then, will be primarily Messianic. And, although it would be fair to say (*e.g.*, in the case of the prayer at Gethsemane) that Jesus realised in a specially personal way the sonship of the Messiah, it would be unjustifiable to go outside the Messianic experience in interpreting his use of the word Father in relation to God.[3]

ix. 2. The Transfiguration is the typical inci-

---

[1] Mark xi. 25. [2] xiv. 36. [3] *Cf.* p. 195.

dent of the second stage of Jesus' self-knowledge, as the Baptism is of the first. The place and time of the event were perhaps deliberately chosen, in order to impress upon the three chosen disciples the truth of Jesus' Messiahship. The vision probably occurred during prayer,[1] and was not unlike some that are narrated of mediæval saints, *e.g.*, S. Francis of Assisi.[2] But as to the point of greatest interest —what the Transfiguration meant to Jesus himself—there is hardly any indication. The disciples are too much preoccupied with their own feelings to wonder what he may be thinking. One may infer from the fact that he is seen to be talking with Moses and Elijah (typical of the Law and Prophets, and the latter also re-embodied in John the Baptist) that he is meditating on the fulfilment of the Messianic prophecies of the Old Testament in himself. In particular, as S. Luke suggests, he is probably thinking of "his decease which he was about to accomplish at Jerusalem".[3] The fact that the baptismal commission is repeated at this

[1] Luke ix. 29 ; *cf*. Mark vi. 46.

[2] *Eg*. I Fioretti del glorioso messere Santo Francesco e de suoi Frati (ed. Passerini), capit. xvi.

[3] Luke ix. 31.

moment of Transfiguration—unless it be due merely to assimilation—is probably significant of the importance of the incident to Jesus himself, as inaugurating a new stage in his ministry, with a clearer knowledge of himself, and a more definite foresight of his Passion. But the content of his consciousness remains entirely Messianic.

ix. 19. "O faithless generation, how long shall I be with you? how long shall I bear with you?" may be compared with the parable of the bridegroom in the first part of the ministry.[1] In both cases Jesus is conscious of the coming time of separation. There is a particular appropriateness in its expression here, immediately after the Transfiguration.

ix. 37. "Whosoever shall receive one of such little children in my name, receiveth me; and whosoever receiveth me, receiveth not me, but him that sent me."

The word "sent" in this passage is another way of stating the "came" or "came forth" of two previous passages.[2] It refers, like them, to the special mission of which Jesus was

---

[1] Mark ii. 19, above.
[2] i. 38, ii. 17; cf. x. 45, below.

conscious. Like them, it cannot safely be made to mean anything more.

In any case this is the main teaching of the passage—that Jesus represents God in the same kind of way as the child represents Jesus. In what kind of way is that? The clue to the meaning of the passage seems to be given by the word "receive". It is used in two very similar senses in the second Gospel—of receiving the Kingdom of God, and of receiving those who preach the Gospel of the Kingdom. Thus it can only be used of the child in this case if the child be taken as a type of the disciples—an interpretation of the passage which S. Matthew actually embodies in his version of it.[1] And the meaning will be that, in listening to the preaching of the disciples, men will be listening to Jesus, and that, in listening to Jesus, they will be listening to the teaching of God. This is Jesus' own account of the "authority" that his hearers had found so noticeable in his teaching and action.[2] There were many things in the counsels of God about which he never spoke, and some about which he admitted himself to be unable to speak; but wherever he undertook to

[1] Matt. xviii. 3.   [2] Mark i. 22, 27, etc.

speak he did it with certainty and confidence, knowing himself to be right. Such is the claim of the present passage.

x. 17. This important passage has already been dealt with in another connection.[1] Its bearing upon the present inquiry lies not so much in the meaning of that "goodness" which Jesus declines to attribute to himself, as in the relationship which he implies between himself and God. The language is not Messianic. There is no use of the titles Father or Son. And a broad distinction is drawn—a distinction which cannot reasonably be confined to the single ground of "goodness"—between Jesus and God. That this idea admits of reconciliation with that (for instance) of the last passage, cannot be doubted, though there may be some difficulty in bringing them together. In Jesus' self-knowledge both were true experiences. In our account of him neither can be omitted.

x. 40. This is one of those instances in which Jesus admits the limitation of his knowledge and power. "To sit on my right hand and on my left hand is not mine to give : but it is for them for whom it hath been prepared." S. Matthew adds the unspoken conclusion, "of my

[1] *Cf.* p. 159.

Father," [1] and brings out the essential likeness of this passage to the last. Both explain points of difference between Jesus and God. But whereas that dealt with the question from the moral point of view, this approaches it from the side of knowledge and prerogative. It is not merely that the formal arrangements of the Kingdom (if we may so say) are not in Jesus' hands. It is also implied that he does not himself know for whom "it hath been prepared," and therefore would in any case be unable to act. It is an important fact that these limitations are brought into direct contact with the idea of the Kingdom, and are shown to have formed part of the Messianic consciousness. Thus, in the light of the present passage, it becomes easier to interpret the last, and to combine the rather divergent elements that make up Jesus' self-knowledge.

On the whole, then, there is throughout this second period of the ministry a noticeable advance in the extent and depth of the meaning of the Messiahship, as Jesus appears to understand it himself, and to interpret it to his disciples. If the title Prophet is the best summary of the earlier stages of Jesus' consciousness, that of

[1] Matt. xx. 23.

Messiah seems to be best to represent the central period. It remains to be seen what further enrichment comes during the last stage of the ministry.

VIII

x. 45. If any one saying may be taken to mark the transition from the second to the third stage of Jesus' Messianic consciousness, it is this—"The Son of man came not to be ministered unto, but to minister, and to give his life a ransom for many". It is clear from the context that the first meaning of the words is the example of ministry which Jesus sets to his disciples. The rule of their life is to be the same as the rule of his own, namely humility. This in itself is an enrichment of the idea of the Messiahship. But it is combined with an element which is entirely new to the Gospel, and which is expressed by a word used nowhere else in the New Testament.[1] The form that Jesus' ministry takes is to give his life as a ransom,

---

[1] λύτρον, Mark x. 45 = Matt. xx. 28 (an exact reproduction). Luke omits the saying, but keeps the corresponding words λύτρωσις and λυτροῦσθαι in connection with the "redemption of Israel" expected by pious Jews, and looked forward to in the person of Jesus (i. 68, ii. 38, xxiv. 21).

JESUS HIMSELF

that is, to give it in exchange for the lives of men. From a previous passage[1] we may infer that the giving of life means primarily death: but it perhaps need not exclude the interpretation that Jesus' whole ministry was a ransom. The essential element, self-sacrifice, is the same throughout. "Ransom" is a fairly common idea in the Old Testament, and would have been understood by Jesus as meaning the price paid for a life that had been forfeited,[2] or as a security against future forfeiture.[3] It is on these lines that we must choose between the various theories of "ransom" that have been propounded. In what respect Jesus supposed the "many" lives to have been forfeited, or to be in danger of forfeiture, the passage does not state; nor in what way he imagined that his life could be accepted in redemption of those. The saying stands alone, and gains no more than indirect support from other passages in the gospel. That it belongs to the Messianic consciousness

---

[1] Mark viii. 35.

[2] *E.g.* the criminally careless owner of a dangerous animal shall be sentenced to death, but may commute his sentence by a money payment, Exod. xxi. 28.

[3] *E.g.* the half-shekel "atonement money," Exod. xxx. 11; *cf.* Matt. xvii. 24.

is shown by the use of the title "Son of man"; as also the fact that it is as man that Jesus is able to give his life as surety for men's lives. But beyond this general conclusion it is difficult to go.

x. 46. The blind man of Jericho, Bartimæus, addresses Jesus repeatedly as "Son of David". Jesus at the time makes no comment upon this, doubtless accepting it as a popular Messianic title. But on a later occasion he disputes the scribes' exegesis of Psalm cx., upon which the Messianic meaning of the title was based; and he does so, apparently, because he believes himself to be the Messiah, but does not believe himself to be descended from David.[1] There is no reason to doubt that such was his state of mind on the present occasion too.

xi. 1. The typical act of the third period of the ministry, corresponding to the Baptism and the Transfiguration, is the entry into Jerusalem. Like those events, it is marked by a pronouncement of Messianic language from the Old Testament—" Hosanna; Blessed is he that cometh in the name of the Lord:"[2] to which are added the words: " Blessed is the kingdom that cometh,

[1] Mark xii. 35, below.
[2] Psalm cxviii. 25.

JESUS HIMSELF

the kingdom of our father David : Hosanna in the highest ". Here " Hosanna " is a prayer for salvation, addressed to Jesus as King, and " the kingdom of our father David " is the Messianic Kingdom in its more material form. The words " in the highest " seem to be a prayer that the " Hosanna " may be answered in heaven. The language is throughout Messianic ; and the only special characteristic of the incident is that Jesus for the first time not merely tolerates, but seems to encourage the appeal to his power and the publication of his claims. The " triumphant " entry is premeditated. The time for concealment is past. The claim is at last to be made that can only lead to the death of the claimant.

xi. 27. When his authority is questioned, during the last week of the ministry, Jesus shows quite clearly that it is " from heaven ". His own authority stands or falls with that of the Baptist. If John was Elijah the fore-runner, Jesus must be the Messiah. The refusal to state explicitly his authority is not a mere retort ; it is an argument. Hitherto Jesus has not argued : that he does so now shows a new urgency in his preaching. But the message is the same as before.

xii. 1. In the parable of the vineyard Jesus represents himself under the image of " the beloved son" of the lord of the vineyard, who represents God. Further, he seems to contrast himself with the Jewish prophets: they are "servants," he is the Son, the heir. When we contrast this passage with that, for instance, in which Jesus calls himself a prophet,[1] we see what a great advance there has been in the Messianic consciousness. As Messiah, Jesus now knows himself to stand in a much more intimate relation to God than do the prophets. They had claimed for God the first fruits of Jewish life. He has come to claim not merely the first fruits, but the whole inheritance. The Messiah is heir to the Jewish Church and nation. They belong to him by right of his relationship to God, and of his mission from God. He claims their surrender. The claim is a very serious one, in view of the position held by the prophets in common estimation: but it is a necessary part of the claim to the Messiahship. And it would be unjustifiable to go outside the Messianic idea for its explanation, especially in dealing with a passage which is throughout metaphorical.

xii. 10. The quotation from Scripture with which the parable of the vineyard is rounded off brings out the same claim to uniqueness in a

[1] Mark vi. 1, above.

rather different way. Jesus stands in the same relation to the Jewish nation as that nation stood to the world — the "head of the corner," the supreme witness to God, the culmination which explains and unifies the whole process of development. The metaphor, and its national interpretation, were so well known to Jesus' audience, that it would have been difficult to express his Messianic claim in a more emphatic or unmistakable way.

xii. 35. There follows another instance of Scriptural exegesis dealing with the Messianic idea. The passage in question is the opening of the 110th Psalm—"The Lord said unto my Lord, Sit thou on my right hand, till I make thine enemies the footstool of thy feet".[1] This had always been interpreted Messianically. Jesus wishes to show that, if so interpreted, it contains an idea fatal to the conventional notion of the Messiah. David, in the psalm, calls the Messiah "Lord": how then can the Messiah be, as is popularly supposed, David's son? There are here several points of interest. (i) In the first place, unless the psalm is by David, Jesus' argument from it breaks down. And most probably it is not by David. (The argu-

[1] Ps. cx. 1.

ment was in any case a purely verbal one : but it was such as would appeal both to Jesus and to his hearers.) (ii) However, the interesting point remains that Jesus should have wished to use such an argument—should have been anxious to prove that the Messiah need not be David's son. The genealogies prefixed to the first and third gospels assert that Jesus *was* descended from David. But apparently he himself knew nothing of this. He had indeed been acclaimed more than once as the Son of David ; but the title had been given, and he had accepted it, as no more than a popular inference from his Messiahship. And it was this wrong inference (as he took it to be, in the light of his own non-Davidic descent) that he now wished to dispute. We infer, then, that Jesus had strong grounds for thinking that he was not descended from David. There would have been no need to raise the question otherwise.[1] (iii) But there is another point. The present saying carries on the argument of the last but one.[2] There Jesus, as Messiah, was shown to stand closer to God than the prophets did. Here he claims to be, not David's son, but his Lord. It is not merely a personal claim. It is a new idea of the

[1] *Cf*. p. 26.   [2] Mark xii. 1, above.

Messiahship. It recognises that the psalm is truer than the popular interpretation of it, and looks forward to a Messiah who is more than an earthly king. And as we inferred from Jesus' questioning of the ordinary interpretation that he thought himself not to be a descendant of David, so we may infer from his insisting on the larger meaning of the psalm that he was conscious of himself as being in some way greater than David.

xiii. 1. The apocalyptic discourse in the second gospel has already received separate treatment.[1] But with reference to Jesus' self-knowledge some points must be reconsidered here. (i) In the first place, Jesus is quite certain that at some future time a great event will happen which will include the passing away of the present material heaven and earth, his own return into the world from some other existence, "trailing clouds of glory," to gather his followers together, and the establishment of the Kingdom of God as a new heaven and earth, an eternal immaterial existence. These ideas in themselves are sufficiently perplexing. It is the more difficult to arrive at their true meaning, whether for Jesus or for the Church, when we consider the

[1] *Cf.* Chap. iv. § vi.

numerous and diverse apocalypses which were current in Jewish thought at this time, and the figurative language in which they were commonly expressed.

(ii) But secondly, there is this paradox. Side by side with the extraordinary personal claim which is made by the idea of the Parousia—a claim in which Jesus places himself, as Son, above the angels, and only a little lower than God—appears the admission of his own ignorance as to the time of this event of which he is so certain. It might be said, perhaps, that the ignorance is one of detail—as to the exact date, within a specified period which is *not* unknown. But this only brings us face to face with the real crux, which is that as the result of Jesus' teaching (of which the present passage is a more or less casual reminiscence, and which we could in fact reconstruct without any such record) the disciples did for many years expect and wait for the second coming—*and it never happened*. It is, of course, possible to suppose that the disciples as a whole quite misunderstood Jesus' teaching on this subject. Or it is possible to think that, in some way which at present we cannot explain, Jesus himself was mistaken. The matter is perhaps not of such importance that we need hesitate to accept either of these alternatives. What is impossible is to deny that, as the result of their intercourse with Jesus, the disciples expected his speedy return, the end of the world, and the establishment of the Kingdom of God.

The whole matter is a very difficult one. One may guess that it is one of those problems the full bearing of which upon the Christian conception of Christ has yet to be realised. Indeed, the discussion of the intellectual limitations involved in the Incarnation has hardly yet begun.

xiv. 22. We shall hardly be wrong in assuming that on the last evening of his life on earth Jesus was supremely conscious of his Messiahship. The Last Supper, the Prayer of Gethsemane, and the isolated words during the Passion and Crucifixion, ought to contain what is really essential in Jesus' self-revelation. With regard to the first of these—an incident too full of meaning to be more than touched on here—two things must be said. The primary fact of which Jesus is conscious during the Last Supper is the nearness of his death, and of the Kingdom that is to be won by his death. He thinks of his betrayal as an event long foretold and predestined—"the Son of man goeth, even as it is written of him": the central act of the Supper becomes a memorial of the death which he is about to die—" this is my body . . . this is my blood ": the present gathering of friends, and the sharing of the cup, are to be repeated, at some time beyond death, " in the kingdom of heaven ". Nothing could be more real and vivid than Jesus' sense of the crisis that is at hand.

But there is another side to this consciousness. That sense of the meaning of his death which we have already traced in a previous saying—" The Son of man came . . . to give his life a ransom for many "—reappears in its final form—" This is my body. . . . This is my blood of the covenant, which is shed for many." The metaphor is of course not quite the same in the two passages. In the earlier saying Jesus seems to regard his death as an exchange for lives that have been forfeited, or that are in danger of forfeiture. In the words of institution his death is a ratification of a covenant [1] made between God and man. The general meaning of these metaphors must be, first, that men's lives are, or will be, forfeit through sin, and that the giving of Jesus' life avails to cancel this forfeiture ; and secondly, that a new law has been given by God to man, and that Jesus' death is man's pledge that he

[1] See Exod. xxiv. 8.

will observe it. (The eating and drinking of the body and blood correspond to Moses' sprinkling of the people with the blood of the old covenant.)

Side by side, then, with Jesus' growing sense of the nearness of his passion, comes an increasing apprehension of its inner meaning. His death had always seemed to him to be the price of the Kingdom: afterwards it became also the ransom of many lives: now at last it is the ratification of a new understanding between God and man. It satisfies three great needs—the need of a life beyond death, the need of a remedy for sin, and the need of divine help to obey a divine law. It is with no lower estimate of his death that Jesus comes to die.

xiv. 32. If at the Last Supper we get Jesus' fullest revelation of himself to his disciples, it is in the prayer of Gethsemane that we learn most about his relation to God. He speaks to God as his Father—" Abba, . . . all things are possible unto thee "—assuming the same close relationship as on a previous occasion.[1] But he is quite sure of the reality and independence of his own will—" not what I will, but what thou wilt ". He states a duality, and annuls it in the

[1] Mark viii. 38, above.

very statement; for his own will is to conform to God's will in everything. Jesus had no theory of the relation of the human and divine will, as theologians have. His words simply represent his common experience — "God wants this; I want that; but I want still more to do what God wants". It is only from dogmatic presuppositions that any difficulty can arise here.

xiv. 61. Passing by some further indications of what has already been established—Christ's vivid sense of his coming death—we find in Jesus' answer to the High Priest a simple avowal of his Messiahship, and a last prophecy of his Parousia. The high priest's question shows that "the Christ" was popularly regarded as "the Son of the Blessed": his reception of Jesus' answer makes it clear that the blasphemy lies in claiming to be the Messiah, not in claiming anything not covered by that title. The public announcement of this claim, for the first time, seems horrible to the high priest, blasphemy "worthy of death".

xv. 2. The reply to Pilate is different. The question is a political one. Does Jesus claim to be "the King of the Jews," as his enemies suggest? (As a matter of fact the second gospel omits the steps which led up to the putting of this question : the title occurs here for the first time.) Jesus' answer is ambiguous. It is the religious claim, and that alone, with which he is concerned.

xv. 34. Jesus' life ends with a cry which, for all that it is a quotation from a psalm, is a cry of personal distress and despair. Was this really his last experience—a doubt of the presence of God who had been so near to him all his life? Or did his consciousness end, as the psalm ends, in a vision of the victory of the cross, and the coming of the Kingdom—" All the ends of the earth shall remember and turn unto the Lord : and all the kindreds of the nations shall worship before thee. For the Kingdom is the Lord's : and he is the ruler over the nations "—?[1]

IX

Certain conclusions may now be formulated, as the result of our examination of the foregoing evidence.

(i) In the first place we may claim to have verified, so far as it is possible, the hypothesis of the gradual growth of Jesus' self-conscious-

[1] Psalm xxii. 27.

ness with which we set out. Granted that the boundaries of the separate stages cannot be exactly determined, yet it remains true in the main that at the beginning of his ministry Jesus regarded himself primarily as a Prophet, during the central period as the Messiah, and during the closing weeks as in some sense the Redeemer of mankind. Up to the time of Peter's profession of faith he knew himself, one may venture to guess, as one consecrated and commissioned by God for a special work in the world—the preaching of the Kingdom of God. From the time of the Transfiguration onward it seems clear that his mind was more and more preoccupied with the idea of the Messiahship, and that he was gradually accumulating the new content of that idea, in his anticipation of suffering and death. Finally it seems to have been only in the last weeks of his life that Jesus felt the full meaning of his death, as the ransoming of men from sin, and the pledge of their new relationship to God.

(ii) Secondly, the titles into which Jesus translated his personality, or by which his followers acclaimed him, were drawn from recognised Messianic sources. This shows that Jesus believed himself to be the Messiah, and taught his disciples (though only in the later part of the ministry) that he was so. But it does not exclude what we find to be the crux of his teaching —a new interpretation of the Messiahship. This interpretation takes three forms—(a) the Kingdom is to be won by the suffering and death of the Messiah : (b) the Messiah's death is to ransom such lives of his followers as have been or will be forfeit on account of sin : and (c) it is to be a pledge of a new covenant between God and man, in which a higher law is ordained than that of Sinai, and a nearer presence of God assured than in the tabernacle of the wilderness.

(iii) Thirdly, "the Son of man" is the title which most often represents to Jesus himself the person that he feels himself to be, and the work that he has set himself to do. It is as typical or representative man that he meets his greatest spiritual experiences. But, as Messiah, he is also "Son of God"; and this Sonship is to him a personal relationship, which does not, indeed, in any way impair the independence and freedom of his mind and will, but which involves perfect harmony and co-operation, as between Father and Son.

Who, then, did Jesus think himself to be?

The formal answer is a simple one. He thought himself to be the Messiah. And what did he understand by that? He understood, first, what his fellow-countrymen understood by it—the conception of the Anointed one, the Son of God, foretold by the prophets, the fulfilment of his nation's hopes, the founder of the Kingdom of God. And, secondly, he held this belief about himself in a way that it had never been held before. He thought that after death he would rise again. He thought that after rising again he would return in a glorified state at the end of the present world to inaugurate a new existence. He thought that his Passion was prevalent with God to ransom men from the power of sin. He thought that his Gospel was God's new law for men. He thought that his death was a pledge of their conversion, a security for their struggle towards holiness.

All this, on the strictest treatment of the evidence, is contained in the earliest and most certain gospel, in the recollections of Jesus' oldest friend. If Jesus did not think of himself thus, the gospel is utterly mistaken in its representation of him—we can neither trust this, nor, *a fortiori*, any other extant account of the Incarnation. If he did think of himself thus, he was either right in doing so, or he was deluded. If he was deluded, with however sincere and devout a misunderstanding, the whole character of the Christian religion is changed. If he was thinking truly, then his experience has been rightly taken by the Christian Church as a fact unique in the religious history of the world.

CHAPTER IX

CONCLUSION

I BEGAN this inquiry with no other intention than that of gathering materials for a description. But as I look back through the evidence I find that the description has gradually grown into an argument. I set out to discover, if it were possible, some first-hand testimony as to how Jesus spoke and thought and lived among men, expecting it to be fragmentary and indecisive. I find myself now, from the cumulative force of the evidence, framing a formula for the Incarnation.

My starting-point was the hypothesis (for which I considered myself to have sufficient grounds in experience) that the second gospel represents on the whole an early and authentic account of the life and death of Jesus—not a complete account, of course, but an adequate one, in which nothing essential is omitted or misrepresented.

The canon of criticism which seemed to me to follow from this was that one should prefer

CONCLUSION

the primary or literal meaning of the principal document, taken in isolation, to any secondary interpretation of it derived from comparison with other and inferior authorities.

At first the trend of the evidence seemed to be almost entirely in one direction. Whatever aspect of the life of Jesus came under inquiry, the witness always seemed to lay most stress upon the complete humanity of his hero—upon the thoroughness with which he shared the common experiences of family life and class and nationality; upon his social and intellectual outlook, so intimately affected by his circumstances; and upon the temper of morality and religion which marked him out a Jew.

But by degrees I found that my witness was beginning to speak in a rather different strain. Without in any way lessening his emphasis on the complete humanity of Jesus, he was yet representing it in an increasingly unfamiliar way. He described to me a person who for thirty years was so given to home life that he threw it up in a moment to become a homeless wanderer; who, without any special education, spoke in such a way that well-to-do men abandoned their trade to become beggars for him, and crowds left their villages to sit at his feet in the desert; who was able to work at will and "by the light of nature" such changes of body and mind as science is barely beginning to explain; who soberly believed himself to be the fulfilment of inspired prophecies, and of the age-long expectation of his people; who deliberately courted a shameful death in order to win for his friends a kingdom not of this world; and who held that his self-sacrifice would redeem mankind from the power of sin, and establish them in a new relationship towards God.

These things would have been sufficiently surprising if they had been related of a wholly miraculous and unapproachable being. That they should be said and believed about that Jesus whom I already knew to have lived as man among men, supping with publicans and sinners, disputing with scribes in the Temple, and hanging naked on the cross,—this seemed to make them so incredible that they must be true.

And so, I argued, it was because the disciples knew Jesus as man that they were ready to worship him as divine. They knew him as a single person: there was no disunity between act and act, thought and thought: all his faculties and habits of body, mind, and will were one self.

They knew that he grew as a whole : bodily form, thought, and spiritual experience alike passed through stages from less to greater maturity. They knew that his humanity was real and complete and local : that the Jewish features and Galilean speech involved the Jewish, Galilean, and Nazarene "point of view" in all its essential elements. Yet they knew that there was more in him than this—a great power of mind and speech, a simplicity of goodness, a close familiarity with the ways of God : and, as their experience of him grew, it was in these things that they found Jesus himself : they followed him less as Messiah than as Master, they revered him less for his public miracles than for his private teaching, they thought less of what he did, and wondered more at what he was. For them, as for himself, the Resurrection intervened between the old life and the new. But his new existence would have been meaningless without the mortal life that preceded it. And the disciples came to worship him as God, not in spite of, but because of their experience of him as man.

This, then, is the first conclusion towards which I am led by the evidence of the second gospel—that Jesus is a single person, who *as a whole* lives a human life, and *as a whole* can be worshipped as divine. There is no possible or desirable division between what is human in him and what is divine. The human in him *is* divine. When he is most truly man, then he is most truly God.

To this I am bound to add the idea of *growth*, which, if there be no distinction within the person of Jesus, must also apply to him, somehow, *as a whole*.

And lastly—as to the content of this single growing personality—I am convinced that I shall be making a fatal mistake if I rest belief in Jesus' divinity upon the powers which appear on the surface of his life rather than upon the character that underlies them. It is a misunderstanding of the gospels to think that it is by works of healing, or signs of power, as such, that Jesus claims the homage of the world. It is not by these, but by his personal appeal—by the power of his mind and the love of his heart, working themselves out in friendship and self-sacrifice, limited by, and yet always transfiguring, the forms in which they were set. If men cannot hear this appeal, it is idle to speak to them of lesser miracles.

This might be a puzzling conclusion, if I already knew at all fully what I mean by "man" and "God," and how they ought to be related in an "Incarnation". But it is only in the life and death of Jesus that I come to understand the meaning of these terms. So I am content to say of the whole person of Jesus, "This is what I mean by man," and again, "This is what I mean by God". The better I know him, the better I shall be able to understand what God is, and what man is, and how it is possible that they should meet in him. At present I am no more than at the edge of the mystery.

Thus far S. Mark's gospel, as I am able to understand it. I think that it contains the essence of the experience and formulas of the Church. Certainly it is necessary to apprehend Jesus by faith as well as by reason; and it is only by learning to do his will that I shall come to understand at all fully who he is. But I believe that it was by the experience of his humanity that the disciples came to understand and worship his divinity. And I expect that the same method is the truest for us all.

INDEX TO REFERENCES TO S. MARK

Ref.	Page	Ref.	Page
i. 4-5	41	ii. 5	58, 65, 172
8	185	6-7	177
9	18	8	77, 187
9-11	236	10	57
10	21, 61, 186, 243	12	23
11	31, 87	14	232
12	21, 61, 186, 243	14-17	113
12-13	42	15	30, 62
13	90, 143	15-17	45
14	21, 32	16	153, 177
15	21, 32, 132	17	151, 241
17	232	18	153
18	29, 61	18-22	175
20	29, 61	19	37, 232, 242, 252
21	61, 174	20	78
22	23, 76, 253	21	36
23	58, 61	21-22	113
24	18, 91, 181, 238, 246	22	36
25	55, 213	23	153
27	23, 76, 114, 253	23-28	45, 175
29	30, 61	25	242, 247
30	58, 61	26	84, 177, 190
33-35	61	27	46
34	55, 92, 181, 239	28	181
35	69	iii. 1	18
38	52, 240	1-4	107, 175
40	172	5	65, 66, 153
41	59, 64, 143	10	208
43-44	55	10-11	58
44	174, 176	11	181, 239
45	62	11-12	92
ii. 1	30	12	55
1-4	62	14	233
1-12	156	15	93
3-12	44	16-17	112
4	30	19	30

Ref.	Page	Ref.	Page
iii. 20	21, 62	v. 28-29	187
21	22	29	172
22	177, 178	30	59, 187
22-30	93, 186	31	62
23	91	32	66
26	91	34	58
27	37, 47, 91	35	223
28	67, 243, 244	37	55, 69
28-29	156	39	100, 224
28-30	178	40	55, 145
31	24	41	67
31-32	62	42	125
34	66	43	36, 55
34-35	24	vi. 1	244, 246, 260
35	190	2	25, 76, 174
iv. 1-11	90	3	24, 25, 34, 182
2-9	48	4	182, 244
3-9	38	5	172
9	54, 67	5-6	58
10-12	49	6	65
10-13	53	7	93
11	132	7-13	53
15	90	8	146, 170
21	36, 151	8-9	32
22	46, 151	11	37
24	36, 47	13	93
25	47	14	101, 182
26-28	38	15	182
26-29	47, 48, 130, 133	16	101, 182
30-32	133	30-31	32
31-32	38, 130	31	62
33-34	50, 53	34	64, 144
35-39	212	35	220
35-41	170	35-38	129
38	69	37	59
41	181	38	146
v. 2	58	41	66
3-5	95	43	146
6-12	92, 95	45	63
7	181, 239	45-50	215
10	94	45-52	212
10-17	147	46	69, 251
11-12	95	48	59, 64
12-13	94	56	58, 60, 187, 208
18-19	112	vii. 1-8	175
19	56, 151, 195	2	153
22-23	59	5-17	50

INDEX TO REFERENCES

Ref.	Page	Ref.	Page
vii. 6-13	105	viii. 35	47, 257
9-13	145, 175	36-37	150
10	85	38	79, 101, 195, 231, 233, 247, 267
13	190	ix. 1	99, 133
14-23	50, 141, 154	2	69, 250
17-23	53	4	87
18-19	36	5	231
20-23	131	9	183, 231, 247
21	142	9-13	52
22	156	11-13	32, 178
24	63	12	52, 79, 247
24-30	116	13	101
25	125	14	178
28-29	65	18	93, 95
29	172	19	65, 78, 171, 252
31	221	20	95
32	59	21-24	145
34	66, 67	23	171, 172
36	56	23-24	58
43	221	24	125
viii. 1	69	25	55
1-5	129	28	93
2	59, 64, 144	29	95, 171
2-3	221	30	63
5	146	31	52, 79, 183, 231, 247
8	146	33	30
10	63	33-34	68
11	179	35	69, 152
12	65	35-36	69
13	63	35-41	53
14	146	36	65, 125, 144
15	179	36-37	53
16-17	69	37	125, 195, 233, 252
17-21	170	38-40	94, 151
22	59	39	233
22-23	144	40	47
23	55, 65, 69	41	36
26	56	42	36, 125, 149
27	63, 230, 245	42-47	155
27-30	52	43-47	102, 134, 150, 152
27-34	51, 68	43-48	131, 157
28	101	49-50	103
29-30	182	50	36, 144
31	52, 79, 176, 183, 230, 231, 246	x. 1	63
33	91, 143, 149, 191	2	179
34	37, 152, 233	2-9	86, 123

Ref.	Page	Ref.	Page
x. 3	85	xi. 18	114
10	30	20-25	217
11-12	123	21	217
14	234	22	192
15	67, 125, 130, 134, 152	22-24	171
16	65, 125, 144	22-25	53
17	254	25	144, 155, 195, 250
17-18	160	27	259
17-22	106, 117	27-33	32, 115, 184, 229
17-30	134	xii. 1	38, 259, 262
18	193, 196	1-9	48, 194, 195, 231
21	64, 66, 112, 129, 147	1-12	184
23	66	10	260
23-25	118	10-11	46, 87, 231
23-31	53	12	115
24	70	13	179
25	39	13-15	126
27	191, 196	13-17	45, 106, 107, 118
29	67, 117, 125, 152, 234	14	127, 151, 180
29-30	118	15	77
32-42	69	15-17	127
33	52, 183, 231, 247	17	191
33-34	79	18-25	124
35-40	29, 135, 183, 231	18-27	45, 86, 106, 179
35-45	106	24	190, 196
38	78, 152, 234	26	85
39	231	26-27	46, 105, 196
40	101, 194, 254	28-34	45, 153, 178
42	116	29	196
42-45	53	34	112, 136
43	152	35	258, 261
45	183, 256	35-37	27, 46, 87, 88, 105, 178, 184
46	63, 258		
47	18	35-40	115
52	58	36	85, 186
xi. 1	258	38-39	37
2	37	38-40	178
3	147, 231	41-42	70
7-10	231	41-44	104, 119
8-9	63	43	69
10	52, 135, 184	xiii. —	98, 136
11	114	1	263
12-14	38, 161, 217	3	70
14	212, 218	3-4	45
15	114	10	78, 99
15-18	115, 148	11	186
17	174	15-16	36

INDEX TO REFERENCES

Ref.	Page	Ref.	Page
xiii. 17	145	xiv. 30	78, 143
17-18	36	32	267
19	190	32-35	169
20	194	33-34	69
24-27	39	33-39	143
26	79, 102, 184	36	67, 193, 195, 196, 250
27	102	38	142, 143, 187
28-29	38	44	114
30	99	48	37
30-31	80	50-52	114
32	100, 193, 249	61	268
xiv. —	114	61-62	184, 195
3-9	119, 231	66-72	114
4-5	146	67	18
5	129	xv. —	137
9	78	2	268
10	176	3	176
13	36	10	176
14	147, 231	11	176
21	150, 231	31	176
22	265	34	67, 143, 196, 269
22-24	232	43	137
22-25	52	xvi. 6	18
25	102	7	114

INDEX TO SUBJECTS

Subject	Page
Acts, Account of Jesus in	8
Apostles, their call	29
— social relations with Jesus	68
— social status of	111
Asceticism	153
Authority	76
— of Old Testament	85
Authorship of O.T. books	85
Birth	19, 26
Blasphemy	156
Books, Favourite	84
Characteristic acts	66
Charity	129
Children, Treatment of	125
Christianity, a historical religion	3
— nature of its witness to Jesus	4
Claims, Personal	229
Creeds	15, 16
Criticism, textual	5
— literary and historical	6
Demonology	89
Devils, Power over	92
Discipleship	232
Emotion	64, 143
Eschatology	96
Evangelistic zeal	150
Evil, Personal power of	90
Faith	169
— its part in miracles	57, 172, 205

Subject	Page
Family life	122, 144
Forgiveness	155
Future life	100
God, Idea of	188
Gospels, method of study	2
— origin	10
— interrelation	12
— apocryphal	17, 26
— trustworthiness	74
Hell	102
Holy Spirit	185
Humility	152, 167
Incarnation, Meaning of	39, 70, 72, 107, 138, 162, 196, 228, 272, 274
Insight	77
Ipsissima verba	67
Jerusalem, Knowledge of	113
Jewish Church	173
S. John's Gospel	11
S. John the Baptist	31
Kingdom of God	131, 188
Knowledge, Jesus', of himself	234
— Limitation of	74
Language, of home life	36
— of village	37
— of country	37
S. Mark's Gospel	13
Marriage and Divorce	123

INDEX TO SUBJECTS

Subject	Page
Messianic Consciousness	180, 269
Method of Inquiry	13, 16
Ministry, Early	61
Miracles of healing	201
— "of nature"	210
Moral principles	141
New Testament, its witness to Jesus	6
Old Testament, Jesus' use of	81
Parables	47
Parousia	79, 98, 247, 264
Passion, Predictions of	246
S. Paul's account of Jesus	7
Personal offences	149
Pharisees	178
Political questions	126
Possession	89
Priests	176
Private property	146
Prophetic power	77
Reincarnation	101
Reserve in religion	168
Sadducees	179
Scribes	177
Scripture	81
Sects, Religious	113, 175
Self-sacrifice	152
Sin, Treatment of	153
Sinlessness	157
Social Questions	128
— Reform	130
Teaching, Methods of	43
— public and private	50
Temptation	142
Thought, ways of	104
Tolerance	151
Wealth	116

www.ingramcontent.com/pod-product-compliance
Lightning Source LLC
Chambersburg PA
CBHW050339230426
43663CB00010B/1917